On the Night the Hogs Ate Willie

ON THE NIGHT THE

Edited by

Barbara Binswanger and Jim Charlton

HOGS ATE WILLIE

and other quotations on all things Southern

A DUTTON BOOK

DUTTON
Published by the Penguin Group
Penguin Books USA Inc., 375 Hudson Street,
New York, New York 10014, U.S.A.
Penguin Books Ltd, 27 Wrights Lane, London W8 5TZ, England
Penguin Books Australia Ltd, Ringwood, Victoria, Australia
Penguin Books Canada Ltd, 10 Alcorn Avenue,
Toronto, Ontario, Canada M4V 3B2
Penguin Books (N.Z.) Ltd, 182–190 Wairau Road,
Auckland 10, New Zealand

Penguin Books Ltd, Registered Offices:
Harmondsworth, Middlesex, England

First published by Dutton, an imprint of Dutton Signet,
a division of Penguin Books USA Inc.
Distributed in Canada by McClelland & Stewart Inc.

First Printing, November, 1994
10 9 8 7 6 5 4 3 2 1

LIBRARY OF CONGRESS CATALOGING IN PUBLICATION DATA
On the night the hogs ate Willie : and other quotations on all things
Southern / edited by Barbara Binswanger and Jim Charlton.
p.   cm.
ISBN 0-525-93762-5
1. Quotations, American. 2. Southern States—Quotations, maxims,
etc. 3. Southern States—Humor. 4. Southern States—Popular
culture.   I. Binswanger, Barbara.   II. Charlton, James
PN6081.058   1994
818'.02—dc20   94-16712   CIP

Printed in the United States of America
Set in Perpetua
Designed by Eve L. Kirch

CONTENTS

Contents

My mother, Southern to the bone, once told me, ''All Southern literature can be summed up in these words: 'On the night the hogs ate Willie, Mama died when she heard what Daddy did to Sister.' '' She raised me up to be a Southern writer, but it wasn't easy.

PAT CONROY

Introduction

On the Night the Hogs Ate Willie is like kudzu—it covers the South. (And friend, if you have to ask what kudzu is, you're definitely not from Dixie!) To us, the book is akin to attending a wonderful cocktail party in Charleston or Memphis or New Orleans, a gathering peopled by hundreds of interesting, witty, and opinionated Southerners all expressing their thoughts on a variety of subjects. Crowded around a table of barbecue, grits, okra, and other Southern delicacies are people like William Faulkner, Eudora Welty, Lewis Grizzard, Maya Angelou, Florence King, and Martin Luther King, expounding on everything from the weather, civil rights, and rednecks to politics, Elvis, and football. It gives any reader a sense of the South.

In researching this collection, we noticed that one subject came up again and again, whether the main topic was sports or weather or cheerleading: The effect the South has on the family. This common thread runs throughout the history of the region and transcends race or education or economic level. Somehow the region engenders a stronger sense of family than the rest of the country. That statement might be disputed by natives of Maine or Wisconsin or Oregon, but in the South the feeling is deeper and more complicated. In a very real way we treat the South itself as family. We love it and hate it, defend it and brag about it, try to improve it, and tolerate its eccentricities even while we're embarrassed by them. You'll find quotations that reflect all these attitudes as you browse through *On the Night the Hogs Ate Willie*. And we hope you'll find, too, the humor and passion that is the essence of the Southern experience.

This book took some two years of enjoyable collaboration and research to gather, and there are a number of Southerners—expatriate and otherwise—we'd like to thank for their help. John Shelton Reed was extremely generous with his time, talent, and writing. Linton Weeks at the *Washington Post* hadn't heard from Barbara since high school, but on the strength of a phone call sent bound issues of the now (sadly) defunct, but still wonderful, *Southern* magazine. Thanks as well to Jim Ferguson, Irv Bogatin, Ken Neill at *Memphis* magazine, Ed Weathers, Lenore Binswanger, and Debbie Binswanger. And to Pat Conroy, whose wonderful quotation is the title and embodiment of this book.

BARBARA BINSWANGER AND JIM CHARLTON

ON THE NIGHT THE HOGS ATE WILLIE

TRUE SOUTH

I suggest that the true Southland is that territory within which, when asked by an outsider whether he is a Southerner, the reply almost invariably is "Hell, yes!" This "Hell, yes" line has the advantage of eliminating the ambivalent wishy-washy fringes, and leaving the unquestionably defiant, hard-core Southland.

HAMILTON C. HORTON, JR.

The South is anywhere below the line where restaurants will bring you grits in the morning (and the Deep South is where they bring the grits without asking or being asked.)

FRED POWLEDGE

The Mason-Dixon Line is the dividing line between cold bread and hot biscuit.

KENTUCKY GOVERNOR BOB TAYLOR

Everyone in the South knows who Jefferson Davis was, and this is one thing that distinguishes the South from other parts of the country.

WILLIAM F. BUCKLEY, JR.

The only place in the world where nothing has to be explained to me is the South.   WOODROW WILSON

What is the difference between the South and the rest of America? It was a while before I figured out there isn't any. The South is America. The South is what we started out with in this bizarre, slightly troubling, basically wonderful country—fun, danger, friendliness, energy, enthusiasm, and brave, crazy, tough people.   P. J. O'ROURKE

The South has preaching and shouting, the South has grits, the South has country songs, old mimosa traditions, clay dust, Old Bigots, New Liberals—all of it, all of that old mental cholesterol, is confined to the Sunday radio.   TOM WOLFE

The South as a land of grace and violence, as beauty and the beast, had an irresistible fascination about it.

It was evil and decadent, but it had also bred heroes and dreamers, and it yielded a tenacious sense of hopefulness that kept the world from going home.

JOHN EGERTON

I think paradoxically the South is known for its violence, a good bit of violence, but at the same time there is a certain tolerance and civility toward people and their opinions. WALKER PERCY

The South may not always be right, but by God it's never wrong! BROTHER DAVE GARDNER

The South has a way of closing down over its own like the jars in which we once captured fireflies out on the veranda. SHARON MCKERN

I happen to know quite a bit about the South. Spent twenty years there one night.   DICK GREGORY

No less than Ireland, the South has been a sow with a propensity for eating its children—especially the brighter and more restive among them.
MARSHALL FRADY

> *O magnet-South! O glistening, perfumed South!*
>   *my South!*
> *O quick mettle, rich blood, impulse and love!*
> *Good and Evil! O all dear to me!*
>   WALT WHITMAN, "O Magnet-South!"

I love everything about the South; I even love hate.
BROTHER DAVE GARDNER

I like the South because of the people. They are loyal. Once they love a team, they're fans forever.
DOMINIQUE WILKINS

I live here because I love and hate to live here. . . . I   live   here   because   it   is   the   only   place   I understand. . . . All I know is truckers and hillbilly singers, if you insist on calling them hillbillies, and people who sell plastic Jesuses out on the highway.

PAUL HEMPHILL

We love the South with a fierce, protective passion such as parents have for a crippled child. There is deep in the soul of the South the courage and the courtesy that survived the wounds; the rare, bright flower that was not twisted by defeat or occupation, the intelligence that knows we must move with time and does not want to be let alone.

RALPH MCGILL

To Be a Southerner

Because I was born in the South, I'm a Southerner. If I had been born in the North, the West, or the Central Plains, I would be a human being.

CLYDE EDGERTON

The Southerner is a local person—to a degree unknown in other sections of the United States. The

Southerner always thinks of himself as being from somewhere, as belonging to some spot of earth.

RICHARD WEAVER

The South impresses its image on the "Southerner" —be he Catholic or not—from the moment he is able to distinguish one sound from another.

FLANNERY O'CONNOR

I don't think of myself as a Negro. I'm a Southerner. I just like the Southern way of life.   JULIAN BOND

In a way, I think Southerners care about each other, about human beings, in a more accessible way than some other people.   EUDORA WELTY

It is important for me to be a Southerner generally the same way it's important for a Jew to be a Jew, or whatever else a man might be. . . . I was born into it—the South—and rather than repudiate it, it seems better to me to try to realize the positive benefits there are from the life situation I grew up in.

JAMES DICKEY

Being a Southerner is definitely a spiritual condition, like being a Catholic or a Jew.   RICHARD WEAVER

I think of myself as a Southerner in almost every aspect of my thinking. I have a Southern attitude, a Southern concern about people. I try to be polite— but I also try to hustle. I'm a good manipulator. And I'm patient. That's a good Southern characteristic to have. And another is understanding failure. You've got to understand failure before you can understand success.   PHIL WALDEN

Southerners have a genius for psychological alchemy. . . . If something intolerable simply cannot be changed, driven away, or shot, they will not only tolerate it, but take pride in it as well.

FLORENCE KING

Southerners can never resist a losing cause.

MARGARET MITCHELL

The Southerner always tended to believe with his blood rather than his intellect.   MARSHALL FRADY

Try to remember that, though ignorance becomes a Southern gentleman, cowardice does not.

> LILLIAN HELLMAN, *Another Part of the Forest*

Southerners, like New Englanders, whom I know better, are survivors by temperament. But they use talk instead of taciturnity, zaniness instead of stoicism, as their method of getting by, and that's more fun.

> EDWARD HOAGLAND

What all this means is that when Southerners achieve American norms of behavior, they cease being Southerners. Or conversely, to be Southern, popular culture characters must be eccentric, neurotic, lazy, bloodthirsty, past-worshiping, Jehovah-obsessed, or race-baiting—or a combination of all of the above or worse.

> JACK TEMPLE KIRBY

I happen to think there will always be a Southern character or feeling, which may not even be definable when a town looks like Illinois or anywhere else. It's an attitude towards life, a way of looking at things that may not last long, but I think it will last longer than other places, except possibly New England.

> EUDORA WELTY

FAMILY TIES

I love the character of Southern people, their sense of heritage and continuity, their tie to the soil, to the land. They provide roots for the whole country. Southerners seem to have a greater sense of family and brotherhood than the rest of the country.

DAVID DUKE

In the provincial South . . . family ties rival the rampant kudzu for entanglement and tenacity.

SHARON MCKERN

Southern belles have names that are walking family trees. . . . it doesn't matter where in the South you go, because the entire South seems to be married to one another. In some towns you can find Davis Carlyle Sotheby and her first cousin Sotheby Carlyle Davis and they are both leading tours for the local pilgrimage. MARILYN SCHWARTZ

The word "home" to a Southern man and Southern woman is synonymous with the word "love."

CORNELIA WALLACE

In the South the family is a much more powerful institution than in other portions of the Republic.

DANIEL HUNDLEY, 1860

Southerners make such good novelists; they have so many stories because they have so much family.

GORE VIDAL

NEUROTICS & ECCENTRICS

That strange blend of sadness, comedy, and hysteria seems to have strained the emotional registers of outsiders. If you ventured far enough into the steamy, dangerous South, would you really cross a border into a country inhabited by Big Daddies and Maggies, Blanche Duboises and Amanda Wingfields—all counseled, at occasional intervals by intoxicated Episcopal clergymen? No, not exactly.   EDWIN YODER

My mother's people . . . the people who captured my imagination when I was growing up, were of the Deep South—emotional, changeable, touched with charisma and given to histrionic flourishes. They were courageous under tension and unexpectedly tough beneath their wild eccentricities, for they had an unusually close working agreement with God. They also had an unusually high quota in bullshit.

WILLIE MORRIS

I'm Southern and I know neurotic behavior.

FAYE DUNAWAY

The nice thing about Southerners is the way we enjoy our neuroses.

FLORENCE KING

BARBECUE

Southern barbeque is the closest thing we have in the U.S. to Europe's wines or cheeses; drive a hundred miles and the barbeque changes.

JOHN SHELTON REED

So seriously is barbeque taken in the South that a recent regional survey actually used a type of barbeque sauce as a demographic variable for differentiating among various regions. But if you are Southern, you already know that.   JIM FERGUSON

It comes minced, chopped, sliced, pulled, or clinging to the ribs; on light bread, buns, corn bread, or as an entrée; with sweet, tangy, thick, thin, mild, medium, or hot sauce; topped with coleslaw, onions, pickles, or nothing; accompanied by baked beans, potato salad, sliced tomatoes, corn on the cob, French fries, potato chips, Brunswick stew, burgoo, or hash on rice. In all its myriad combinations, shapes, and tastes, it's a many-splendored comestible with a single name: barbecue (barbeque, Bar-B-Q, B-B-Q).

JOHN EGERTON

[Barbecue is meat that] shall be cooked by direct action of heat resulting from the burning of hard wood or the hot coals therefrom for a sufficient period to assume the usual characteristics . . . which include the formation of a brown crust. . . . The weight of barbecued meat shall not exceed 70 percent of the weight of the fresh uncooked meat.

U.S. DEPARTMENT OF AGRICULTURE

Some legislators were bothered by the penalties, but if you're eating barbecue, you deserve to know exactly what you're getting.

SOUTH CAROLINA STATE REPRESENTATIVE
JOHN "BUBBER" SNOW, on the passage of his
"Truth in Barbecue" bill

Anyone with a lick of sense knows you can't make good barbecue and comply with the health code.

ANONYMOUS BARBECUE PIT OWNER,
Quoted by John Egerton

We North Carolinians, of course, know—we are not taught, we are born knowing—that barbecue consists of pork cooked over hickory coals and seasoned with vinegar and red pepper pods. . . . Elsewhere in the South, cruder tastes sometimes prevail.

TOM WICKER

Somewhat like religious tenets, barbecue sauces are touted as essential while, at the same time, being declared unknowable. KATHLEEN ZOBEL

At the pinnacle of barbecue knowledge where secret sauces deserve to be secret—well, for these places barbecue connoisseurs have a special phrase: "as good as I've ever had." In barbecue conversation that is the ultimate compliment. DAVID DAWSON

The summer picnic gave ladies a chance to show off their baking hands. On the barbecue pit, chickens and spareribs sputtered in their own fat and a sauce whose recipe was guarded in the family like a scandalous affair. MAYA ANGELOU

This is a slow operation. You can't rush it. You have to know how to wait, and when to act—and when the time comes, you have to move fast and then wait some more. It's too tedious for most young people—they don't have the patience for it.

JAMES WILLIS, barbecue pit man

The barbecue addict who is also a seasoned traveler looks only at the parking lot to prejudge a restaurant's product. If pickup trucks are parked beside expensive imports, he knows the barbecue is good because everyone in town eats there.   GARY D. FORD

There may be religious, political, athletic, or sexual images that stir deeper emotion—may be—but nothing in the realm of Southern food is regarded with more passionate enthusiasm by the faithful than a perfectly cooked and seasoned pork shoulder or slab of ribs.   JOHN EGERTON

It would hurt to see barbecue go the way of chili—cross over what I now think of as the Chili Line.
          CALVIN TRILLIN

SOUTHERN CUISINE

I am the first to admit that Brunswick stew, which I think the world of, lacks the mystique of chili. I don't admit for one minute that the Southwest has any notion of real barbecue, but I will admit freely that those

folks out there have generated more mystique around
their chili than Southeasterners like me have around
Brunswick stew.   ROY BLOUNT, JR.

What chowder is in the North, a gumbo is to the
people of the far Southern states, a Brunswick stew
to Virginians, a terrapin to Marylanders, and a Burgoo
to Kentuckians.

> *The Boston-Cooking School Magazine*, 1907

Somehow in rural Southern culture, food is always the
first thought of neighbors when there is trouble. . . .
"Here, I brought you some fresh eggs for breakfast.
And here's a cake and some potato salad." It means,
"I love you. And I am sorry for what you are going
through and I will share as much of your burden as I
can." And maybe potato salad is a better way of saying it.   WILL D. CAMPBELL

Jewish mothers dispense chicken soup; Southern belles
dispense chicken salad.   MARILYN SCHWARTZ

In fact, cookbooks in the South outsell everything but
the Holy Bible.   JACK and OLIVIA SOLOMON

There was fried chicken, as it is fried only in the South, hominy boiled to the consistency where it could be eaten with a fork, and biscuits so light and flaky that a fellow with any appetite at all would have no difficulty in disposing of eight or ten. When I had finished, I felt that I had experienced the realization of, at least, one of my dreams of Southern life.

JAMES WELDON JOHNSON

When it comes to fried chicken, let's not beat around the bush for one second. To know about fried chicken you have to have been weaned and reared on it in the South. Period. JAMES VILLAS

Next to fried food, the South has suffered most from oratory. WALTER HINES PAGE

Dying unexpectedly and dramatically in unusual circumstances feeds the Southerner's warrior complex. Short of an actual battlefield or ambush, we make do with anything at hand. I know dozens of Southerners who grew up hearing some version of the "He just up and died at the table" story. . . . Given the typical Southern groaning board of three or four different

kinds of meat, ten or twelve different kinds of vegetables, and mountains of hot bread dripping with butter, passing to one's reward while eating is to die in
a perfect state of grace.

FLORENCE KING

[Blackbottom pie] is a pie so delicate, so luscious, that
I hope to be propped up on my dying bed and fed a
generous portion. Then I think that I should refuse
outright to die, for life would be too good to re-
linquish.   MARJORIE KINNAN RAWLINGS

The Moon Pie is a bedrock of the country store and
rural tradition. It is more than a snack. It is a cultural
artifact.   *New York Times*, April 30, 1986

Hell, yes, we eat dirt! And if you haven't ever tried
blackened red dirt you don't know what's good!

Roy Blount, Jr.

Many Southern ladies had Negro cooks to help them;
and just how much we owe to their skill I have no
way of knowing except that almost all of the finest
Southern dishes are of their creating, or at least bear
their special touch, and everyone who loves good
cookery should thank them from the bottom of his
heart.   Duncan Hines

He chopped up peppers, mixed them with vinegar and
Avery island salt, put the mixture in wooden barrels
to age, and funneled the resulting sauce into second-
hand cologne bottles.

James Conaway, on Edward McIlhenny's
development of Tabasco

When the taste changes with every bite and the last
bite is as good as the first, that's Cajun.

Paul Prudhomme

A literal translation of the French term *cochon du lait*
is "pig of the milk," but to the people of Acadiana,

that translation is roughly equivalent to a "really great party." C. RICHARD COTTON

Breaux Bridge is in the Atchafalaya basin, which crawls with crawfish; the town holds a crawfish festival every other year, including a crawfish-eating contest and a crawfish race, in which the penchant of the crawfish for setting off in unpredictable directions has been outwitted by designing the race course in the form of a circular target, with the starting gate at the bull's-eye and the finish line at no matter what point on the circumference.

WAVERLY ROOT and
RICHARD DEROCHEMONT

A New York crawfish craver who couldn't make it to the Atchafalaya basin would have to settle for Paris, where crawfish are called *écrevisses,* except by people from Louisiana, who always call them inferior.

CALVIN TRILLIN

Only a Charlestonian intent on being ostracized, or worse, would make she-crab soup with a he-crab.

PHILLIP HAMBURGER

If you like dishes made out of a piece of lettuce and
  groundup peanuts and a maraschino cherry and
marshmallow whip and a banana
You will not get them in Savannah,
But if you seek something headier than nectar and tastier
  than ambrosia and more palatable than manna,
Set your teeth, I beg you, in one of the specialties de
  Savannah.
Everybody has the right to think whose food is most
  gorgeous,
And I nominate Georgia's.

OGDEN NASH

Quite often when confronted with still another restaurant menu that includes the likes of an elaborate
seafood terrine with a delicate sauce, a sautéed fresh

duck foie gras, and a couple of pristine veal medallions perfumed with exotic wild mushrooms, my thoughts drift to crisp Southern fried chicken, short ribs of beef falling off the bone. . . . I try to negotiate the perfectly sculptured, undercooked, tasteless vegetables while entertaining visions of unctuous, flavor-packed Kentucky Wonder green beans that have simmered for hours with pork fat.   JAMES VILLAS

It is time to eat. Here is supper. Black-Eyed peas with Ham Hock . . . Fried Okra . . . Country Corn bread . . . Sweet Potato Pie. . . . You talk of supping with the gods. You've just done it, for who but a god could have come up with the divine fact of okra?

JAMES DICKEY

On a summer evening some years ago, two of the South's most celebrated writers, William Faulkner and Katherine Anne Porter, were dining together at a plush restaurant in Paris. Everything had been laid out to perfection; a splendid meal had been consumed, a bottle of fine Burgundy emptied, and thimble-sized glasses of an expensive liqueur drained. The maître d' and an entourage of waiters hovered close by, ready to satisfy any final whim. "Back home the butter beans are in," said Faulkner, peering into the distance, "the speckled ones." Miss Porter fiddled with her glass and stared into space. "Blackberries," she said wistfully. EUGENE WALTER

More eating of corn bread would, I'm sure, make a better foundation for American literature. The white bread we eat is to corn bread what Hollywood will be to real American literature when it comes.

SHERWOOD ANDERSON

GRITS

Grits is the first truly American food.

TURNER CATLEDGE

Contrary to popular opinion, neither grits nor hominy ever came close to being universally used in the area prior to the Civil War. SAM BOWERS HILLIARD

Sure, sure, I heard of grits. I just actually never seen a grit before.

JOE PESCI, *My Cousin Vinnie*
(screenplay by Dale Launer)

True grits, more grits, fish, grits, and collards.
Life is good where grits are swallered.

ROY BLOUNT, JR.

I am alarmed over the grits situation. . . . You have to ask the waitress to bring you grits. Previously you only had to ask the waitress not to bring you grits. More recently, there has been an even more alarming trend in this regard. At some restaurants, you not only have to ask for grits, but have to pay for them as well. I consider this a sacrilege, as I am quite sure that the Lord never intended for grits to be sold.

CHARLIE ROBINS

DRINK

Where I come from, coke is Coke, dammit, Coca-Cola—brand name, secret formula, and all. Down South it stands for any dark soft drink; for some it is more largely generic still, denoting any soft drink, period.

ED WEATHERS

Memphis martini: Gin with a wad of cotton in it.

FRED ALLEN

The day when the boys who hang around the Red Ace filling station in Cullman, Alabama, walk into Grigsby's Grocery and order an orange pop, we'll know the South is dead.   RICHARD K. THOMAS

People still joke that a man with a crease on the end of his nose must be a heavy imbiber of moonshine because when you drink straight from a Mason jar, the glass rim hits you in the nose.

RAYMOND SOKOLOV

There's three kinds of moonshine: the hugging kind, the kind that makes you sing, and the kind that gives you fifteen fights to a pint.   RAY HICKS

Moonshining has been one of the constant truths about the South for all of these years, right up there with segregation and hard-shell religion.

PAUL HEMPHILL

What you need for breakfast, they say in East Tennessee, is a jug of good corn liquor, a thick beefsteak, and a hound dog. Then you feed the beefsteak to the hound dog.   CHARLES KURALT

We started out using cheesecloth to help extract the mint essence. The problem was, tiny particles of mint would migrate into the liquid. We switched to Hanes Number Two white T-shirts.

> BILL SAMUELS, head of Makers Mark
> Distillery in Kentucky

If there is, as a product of sincere conviction and honest observance of the law, such a reality as the "Dry South," I have yet to see it.

> R. CHARLTON WRIGHT, on Prohibition

Mississippi was a dry state, one of the last in America, but its dryness was merely academic, a gesture to the preachers and the churches. My father would say that the only difference between Mississippi and its neighbor Tennessee, which was wet, was that in Tennessee a man could not buy liquor on Sunday.

> WILLIE MORRIS

Being in a dry county doesn't mean people don't drink. It just means it's against the law to buy and sell it.   ROGER BRASHEARS, spokesperson for Jack Daniel's Distillery

Mississippi will drink wet and vote dry—so long as any citizen can stagger to the polls.
                              ATTRIBUTED TO WILL ROGERS

It took a special breed of man to make moonshine or fly it over the treacherous back roads into Chattanooga and Atlanta with cops on his tail. Southern-style stock-car racing had as its early heroes old boys from the hills, uneducated and daring and in possession of damned good automobiles.   PAUL HEMPHILL

GOOD OLE BOYS

When I was a kid Uncle Remus put me to bed,
With a picture of Stonewall Jackson above my head.
Then Daddy came in to kiss his little man
With gin on his breath and a Bible in his hand.

And he talked about honor and things I should know.
Then he staggered a little as he went out the door. . . .
I guess we're all gonna be what we're gonna be.
So what do you do with good ole boys like me?

BOB MCDILL

If somebody is a solid, reliable, unpretentious, stand-up, companionable, appropriately loose, joke-sharing feller, with a working understanding of certain bases of head-to-head equal footing, you say, "You know, he's a good old boy. . . . A good old boy will take advantage of another good old boy when he has to, and will help him out when he can. He will also take some creative pride in the way he does the one thing and the other and mixes the two together.

ROY BLOUNT, JR.

When people designate somebody as a good ol' boy the sentence has to start something like, "Well, now, Bubba, he may beat his wife some and burn a few barns when he's drankin', and there's that time he shot his little boy's eye out with a BB gun and all that—but he sure is a good ol' boy."

LARRY L. KING

Being a Bubba will make your adversaries underestimate you, and that immediately gives you the advantage.

ANONYMOUS BUBBA,
quoted in *Southern* magazine

Being a "good old boy" was the highest priority of all. If you were intelligent and made straight A's, got along fine with the teachers, and occasionally studied your books, it was necessary that all this be performed, among the boys you "ran around" with, with a certain casualness that verged on a kind of cynicism.

WILLIE MORRIS

The redneck has an outlaw quality that the good old boy lacks, although the distinction is not hard and fast. Some good old boys find that redneckery has a certain appeal, and they take it up, in some phases of the moon.

JOHN SHELTON REED

Duck-hunting was the gentleman's sport; real rednecks were meat-hunters.

WILL D. CAMPBELL

A good old boy . . . is a generic term in the rural South referring to a man . . . who fits in with the status system of the region. It usually means he has a good sense of humor and enjoys ironic jokes, is tolerant and easygoing enough to get along in long conversations at places like on the corner, and has a reasonable amount of physical courage.

TOM WOLFE

A good ole boy is somebody that rides around in a pickup truck . . . and drinks beer and puts 'em in a litter bag. A redneck rides around in a pickup truck and drinks beer and throws 'em out the window.

BILLY CARTER

The tragedy of the redneck is that he chose the wrong enemy.   WILL D. CAMPBELL

Yes, charisma is the middle name of scads of Southern cads.   ROSEMARY DANIEL

Great personal courage, unusual physical powers, the ability to drink a quart of whiskey or to lose the whole of one's capital on the turn of a card without the quiver of a muscle—these are at least as important as possessions, and infinitely more important than heraldic crests. In the South, if your neighbor overshadowed you in the number of his slaves, you could outshoot him or outfiddle him, and in your own eyes, and in those of many of your fellows, remain essentially as good a man as he.   W. J. CASH

There was something in the very atmosphere of a small town in the Deep South, something spooked-up and romantic, which did extravagant things to the imagination of its bright and resourceful boys.

WILLIE MORRIS

PAGEANTS & POM-POMS

When I was growing up in the South it was expected by polite society that one be faithful to God and beauty.

ROBB FORMAN DEW

The South stresses more beauty, more manners, more charisma, more charm. I do not mean to sound chauvinistic, but girls from other parts of the country do not have the class, the beauty, or the charm that our girls have.

MARY FRANCIS FLOOD, beauty pageant coach

There ought to be a different category for Southern girls. They've been doing this since they were born. They're professionals.

NORTHERN CONTESTANT IN
A BEAUTY PAGEANT

Why have so many Southern women engaged in the grueling activity of baton drill teams? Probably, most of us became ''Stars'' or ''Ettes'' because participation gave us something to do during that high social time in Southern towns, football season.

CAROL FLEMING

I've always felt I'm in a depressionproof business. I told a guy, "Listen, you'll sell the boat before you tell your little daughter she can't have two pom-poms and a sweater and do her thing out there if she was elected cheerleader."

LAWRENCE HERKIMER, president
of the National Cheerleaders' Association

SOUTHERN WOMANHOOD

Who has ever heard of "The Midwestern Lady," or "The Northern Belle"?   GAIL GODWIN

Southern women see no contradiction in mixing strength with gentleness.   SHARON MCKERN

The belle is a product of the Deep South, which is a product of the nineteenth century and the Age of Romanticism. Virginia is a product of the eighteenth century. It is impossible to extract a belle from the Age of Reason.   FLORENCE KING

The Southern belle had certain prerogatives that her more ordinary sisters were not granted, but she had won these by her beauty, her spirited veneer, and her ability to manage men without seeming to do so. The art of dissembling perforce became a valuable social asset for a girl. (In this respect the white Southern woman's position was remarkably similar to the Negro's.)   NANCY MILFORD

Negro girls in small Southern towns, whether poverty-stricken or just munching along on a few of life's necessities, were given as extensive and irrelevant preparations as rich white girls shown in magazines.
                                        MAYA ANGELOU

It was all right to make good grades. It was all part of being a good little girl. But to be a great thinker, to have a great talent and pursue it, would cut you right out of the herd. And that was the thing we were most afraid of.   ANNE RIVERS SIDDONS

Lately I've begun to suspect that the Southern girls who got pregnant early, and disappeared from our lives, either had no ambition at all or had easily manageable hair.   ROBB FORMAN DEW

It is a special vanity of Southern women to believe that they are different from other American women.

SHARON MCKERN

Granny wanted a malleable flirt who would heed her advice, a girl cast in the traditional mold, someone delicate and fragile in both body and spirit, a true exemplar of Southern womanhood. Someone, in other words, either sick or crazy.   FLORENCE KING

She was the South's Palladium, this Southern woman, the shield-bearing Athena gleaming whitely in the clouds, the standard for its rallying, the mystic symbol of its nationality in face of the foe.   W. J. CASH

The friend asked why the rebel army had continued to fight when they knew defeat was certain. Senator Williams said the Confederate soldiers were simply afraid to quit and go home because of the women.

GORDON COTTON

The mistress of the Southern manor was required to act like a lady and work like a drudge.

HODDING CARTER II

The Good Ol' Girl cooks, sews, cleans, knits, skis, rides, scouts, refinishes furniture, raises bromeliads and African violets, takes night courses in self-improvement, does a bit of crochet and crewel embroidery, writes occasional poetry of the type that rhymes, and maintains voluminous diaries and scrapbooks.   SHARON MCKERN

For longer than anyone can remember the Southern Lady has been expected to save the raucous South from itself.

WILLIAM COOPER and THOMAS TERRILL

Anybody who wants to learn about the South should get to know her women. They are tough, loving, frail, and powerful. They hold so many of our best secrets.

JAMES DICKEY

Southern women are Mack trucks disguised as powder puffs.   REYNOLDS PRICE

Southern females learn footstamping about as soon as they become steady on their feet, and then it stands them in good stead the rest of their lives. Footstamping is of untold aid in winning arguments with boyfriends and husbands, although since women's lib, it is not as necessary a device as it used to be.

MILDRED JORDAN BROOKS

Even though Southern women have been put down as belles and empty-headed, some of the strongest leadership has come from them. If you go back through the history of Southern women, they had a great deal to with social change. . . . They are great volunteers. You get more volunteers in the South than anywhere.

BETTY BUMPERS

Granny's good works sprang not from Christian charity but from a desire to win for herself that Holy Grail of Southern accolades, ''great lady.''

FLORENCE KING

The Southern lady has long since escaped cultivation on the plantation: Now she grows wild in the suburbs, and seems as well adapted to life there as in her original habitat.   JOHN SHELTON REED

But you know, our women all speak in that low, plaintive way because they are always excusing themselves for something they never did.

MARY CHESTNUT, South Carolinian
Civil War diarist

Tears, sulkiness, hysteria, even girlish temper tantrums were expected of me as a Southern woman, but I had never heard a lady, or even a gentleman, express direct anger.   ROSEMARY DANIEL

I love those slow-talking Southern girls. I was out with a Southern girl last night, took her so long to tell me she wasn't that kind of girl, she was.

WOODY WOODBURY

Memphis children, especially females, almost invariably speak of their fathers as "Daddy," a flirty little word, which, where I come from, is left only to little children and kept women. Here, even stout matrons use it to stand for "Father."   ED WEATHERS

I know so well what becomes of unmarried women who aren't prepared to occupy a position in life. I've seen such pitiful cases in the South—barely tolerated spinsters living on some brother's wife or sister's husband—stuck away in some little mousetrap of a room—encouraged by one in-law to visit another— little birdlike women without any nest—eating the crust of humility all their life.

TENNESSEE WILLIAMS

I have always said that next to Imperial China, the South is the best place in the world to be an old lady.

FLORENCE KING

For a lifetime, I had dreaded gatherings of the women of Mother's family. One's success as a woman was immediately assessed by Southern standards: an added pound, a less flattering hairdo, the state of one's wardrobe were all commented upon, becoming cause and effect of the failed husband, child, or marriage.

ROSEMARY DANIEL

One of the joys of growing up Southern is listening to women argue about whether nervous breakdowns are more feminine than female trouble or vice versa.

FLORENCE KING

I have a theory that Southern madhouses are full of gifted women who were stifled.

ANNE RIVERS SIDDONS

THE MIND OF THE SOUTH

I grew up in a part of the South generally referred to as "deep," an adjective that has metaphysical as well as geographical connotations.   WILLIAM J. GARRY

The Southern mind is not by habit analytical. . . . There seems to exist a feeling that you do not get at the truth of a thing—or that you do not get at a truth worth having—by breaking the thing in pieces. . . . The Southern mind is, on the other hand, synthetic and mythopoetic—it seeks out wholes, representations, symbols.   RICHARD WEAVER

While the rest of American history has been most notable for an eager and nimble application to the possibilities of the moment, it remained the peculiarity of the South that it always seemed somehow vaguely adrift and lost in time.   MARSHALL FRADY

If life in the South seems to move more slowly than it does elsewhere, it may be because Southern women have the good sense to live in two tenses.

SHARON MCKERN

One must realize that certain Southern virtues resulted from historic accident or even from Southern shortcomings as much as from moral superiority. The South's antimaterialism arose in part from its poverty, its distrust of progress partly from its realization that progress would bring painful racial change, even its religious sentiment partly from its rural isolation and lack of exposure to other ways of viewing life.

FRED HOBSON

There is a form of ambivalance that mixes the notion of what you might do with the notion of what might be done to you, a paradox at the heart of the Southern sensibility, that has to do with how we were diverted from choosing the future of our own society.

MADISON SMARTT BELL

The South is the region that history has happened to.

RICHARD WEAVER

The South has had its full share of illusions, fantasies, and pretensions, and it has continued to cling to some of them with an astonishing tenacity that defies explanation. But the illusion that "history is something unpleasant that happens to other people" is certainly not one of them. . . . For the South had undergone an experience that it could share with no other part of America—though it is shared by nearly all the peoples of Europe and Asia—the experience of military defeat, occupation, and reconstruction.

C. VANN WOODWARD

The happiness of the South was very formidable. It was an almost invincible happiness. . . . Everyone was in fact happy. The women were beautiful and charming. The men were healthy and successful and funny. . . . They had everything the North had and more. They had a history.   WALKER PERCY

The past is not dead. It isn't even past.

WILLIAM FAULKNER

THE CIVIL WAR

For one thing, for over two and a half centuries, well before and well beyond the Civil War, the South was, with slavery and then its sequel, absorbed in an interior, collective experience wholly outside the general American sensibility of innocence and rationality and optimism—an experience belonging in fact to an older and direr script about the human condition.

MARSHALL FRADY

The remark has been made that in the Civil War the North reaped the victory and the South the glory.

RICHARD WEAVER

The American Civil War is an experience central to our lives—all Americans, but especially Southerners. . . . The Civil War is our *Iliad*.

SHELBY FOOTE

It's all now you see. Yesterday won't be over until tomorrow, and tomorrow began ten thousand years ago. For every Southern boy fourteen years old, not once but whenever he wants it, there is the instant when it's still not yet two o'clock on that July afternoon in 1863, the brigades are in position behind the rail fence, the guns are laid and ready in the woods and the furled flags are already loosened to break out. . . .   WILLIAM FAULKNER

All we ask is to be left alone.
            JEFFERSON DAVIS, in his Inaugural Address

We may have our own opinions about slavery; we may be for or against the South; but there is no doubt that Jefferson Davis and other leaders of the South have made an army; they are making, it appears, a navy; and they have made what is more than either, they have made a nation.

> BRITISH PRIME MINISTER WILLIAM GLADSTONE,
> in a speech October 7, 1862

I worked day and night for twelve years to prevent the war, but I could not. The North was mad and blind, and would not let us govern ourselves, and so the war came. Now it must go on until the last man of this generation falls in his tracks and his children seize his musket and fight our battles.

> JEFFERSON DAVIS

No, sir, you dare not make war on cotton. No power on earth dares make war upon it. Cotton is king.

> JAMES HENRY HAMMOND,
> to the U.S. Senate, March 1858

Fiddle-dee-dee. War, war, war. This war talk's spoiling all the fun at every party this spring. I get so bored I could scream. Besides, there isn't going to be any war!

> SCARLETT O'HARA, in Margaret Mitchell's
> *Gone with the Wind*

I wish to live under no other government and there is no sacrifice I am not ready to make for the preservation of the Union save that of honor.

ROBERT E. LEE, in the last days
before secession

My husband has wept tears of blood over this terrible war, but as a man of honor and a Virginian, he must follow the destiny of his State.

MRS. ROBERT E. LEE

I just took the shortcut and got there first with the most men.

CONFEDERATE GENERAL NATHAN FORREST,
after capturing Murfreesboro, 1863

Let us determine to die here, and we will conquer. There is Jackson standing like a stone wall. Rally behind the Virginians.

> BARNARD BEE, Confederate soldier,
> said at the First Battle of Bull Run, 1861

The young bloods of the South; sons of planters, lawyers about towns, good billiard players and sportsmen, men who never did work and never will. War suits them. . . . They are splendid riders, first-rate shots, and utterly reckless. . . . These men must all be killed or employed by us before we can hope for peace.   GENERAL WILLIAM TECUMSEH SHERMAN

Some of us fancied that the Southern people were given to vaporing—that each one of them was equal to five Northern soldiers. But the South learned that Paul Revere still rode the highways of Massachusetts, and that the man of Concord still plowed the fields. And we, on our part, learned that the spirit of the cavalier which was found in the Southern army was combined with the reserve and steadfastness of Cromwell's Ironsides.   BENJAMIN HARRISON

The cornfield pea was the only faithful friend the Confederate Army ever had.   ROBERT E. LEE

RECONSTRUCTION

When the smoke and fire is over, the Negroes have nothing gained, the whites have nothing left, while the jackals have all the booty.

RICHARD HARVEY CAIN

He finds his house in ruins, his farm devastated, his slaves free, his stock killed, his barns empty, his trade destroyed, his money worthless; his social system, feudal in its magnificence, swept away; his people without law or legal status; his comrades slain and the burdens of others heavily on his shoulders.

HENRY GRADY, on the returning
Confederate Soldier

As he ate Ritz crackers and sweet butter, he imagined how Richmond might be today if the war had ended differently. . . . Richmond would have five million souls by now, William and Mary would be as good as Harvard and less subverted. In Chattanooga and Mobile there would be talk of the "tough, cynical Richmonders," the Berliners of the hemisphere.

WALKER PERCY

The pain of defeat is something that can be shared by everyone, since everyone at some stage in his life knows defeat of some sort. . . . But the pain of the Confederate Memorial is very great; the defeat it speaks of is complete. Defeat like this leads to religion.

V. S. NAIPAUL

We understand it was the Civil War which made our country what our country is rather than the Revolution. The Revolution started us out, but the Civil War decided which way we were going.   SHELBY FOOTE

In the South the war is what A.D. is elsewhere; they date from it.   MARK TWAIN

There was no Marshall Plan for the South after the war.   WALKER PERCY

In the 1860s and 1870s, when people just like them went West, we called them "pioneers" and "builders of America." If, for the same reasons, they went to Louisiana instead of Kansas, we called them "evil carpetbaggers."   JOHN BOLES

The South sinned. Sinned in her pride, her prosperity, her confidence. Sinned in the way she allowed a few fanatical demagogues to precipitate her into the war. God has humbled her. But strongly as I feel all this, so strongly do I feel that, though we have fallen, we shall rise again. . . . I would rather be the South in her humiliation than the North in her triumph.

CORNELIA SPENCER

There was a South of slavery and secession—that South, thank God, is dead. There is a South of union and freedom—that South, thank God, is living, breathing, growing every hour.

HENRY GRADY, editor of *Atlanta Constitution*, 1888

BLACK & WHITE

The black Southerner and white Southerner are locked to the land and to history, a painful history of guilt and cruelty and ignorance. It clings to us like the moss on the trees.

MAYA ANGELOU

The future of American Negroes is in the South.

W.E.B. DuBois

One third of the population of the South is of the Negro race. No enterprise seeking the material, civil, or moral welfare of this section can disregard this element of our population and reach the highest success. BOOKER T. WASHINGTON

As long as the Negroes are held down by deprivation and lack of opportunity, the other poor people will be held down alongside them.

JAMES (BIG JIM) FOLSOM

Now, young man, you can see some things without me writing them down. I'm not working for equality or anything like that. I figger when you teach niggers to read and write and figger they can kinda look out for themselves—you know, people can't cheat them like they did before.

HUEY LONG, interview with Roy Wilkins

When the Southern white man asks the liberal Caucasian, "Do you want your daughter to marry a nigger?," he is probably hitting the nail on the head, for that is the crux of the entire color problem.

GEORGE SAMUEL SCHUYLER, 1927

I have a dream that one day on the red hills of Georgia the sons of former slaves and the sons of former slaveholders will be able to sit down together at the table of brotherhood. I have a dream that one day even the state of Mississippi, a desert state sweltering with the heat of injustice and oppression, will be transformed into an oasis of freedom and justice. . . . This is our hope. This is the faith with which I return to the South.

MARTIN LUTHER KING, JR.

One hears a good deal about the high social origins of the Southern planters, [and] very many derive indisputably from the first families of England. It is the same blood [that] flows in these mixed colored people's veins. Just think of the sublime absurdity, therefore, of the ban. There are gentlemen of education and refinement, qualified lawyers and doctors, whose ancestors assisted in the Norman Conquest, and they dare not enter a car marked "white."   H. G. WELLS, 1906

In the South it was very ethical, churchgoing men
went home to their wives every night, paid their tax
on time, they were the biggest Jim Crow advocates
in the South. They didn't have anything wrong with
them, other than they hung black people on the week-
ends and ran Jews out of town.

AL SHARPTON

At the time I was growing up, the white Southerner
in the rural and small-town South felt threatened by
blacks. You don't hate what doesn't threaten you. As
long as somebody was below you, you had power.
We were a conquered and occupied people, the only
people in the United States to be like that. And this
—our attitude to blacks—was the only way we could
feel or exercise our power at all.

ANNE RIVERS SIDDONS

I was raised Southern-style—by the maid. No one can
understand the mystery of the South without delving
into this murmuring undertone—a relationship pri-
mordial, like parent and child, of discipline and need,
shadowing every white Southerner throughout the rest
of his life.   ELI EVANS

Something was wrong with a world that tells you love
is good and people are important and then forces you
to deny love and to humiliate people.

LILLIAN SMITH, on growing up in the South

Southerners are the more lonely and estranged, I think
because we have lived so long in an artificial social
system that we insisted was natural and right and
just—when all along we knew it wasn't.

CARSON MCCULLERS

Then, as now, blacks found that homes in the better
neighborhoods were rarely for sale to them, no matter
what rung of the economic ladder they occupied. So
when their white neighbors moved to showing off with
a split-level ranch home in the new suburbs, blacks
kept to cars, demonstrating their financial standing by
buying Cadillacs and Lincolns and Packards. Whites
who didn't understand—and still don't—sneered at
what seemed to them ostentation.   WILLIAM JEANES

You know, I was a social-climbin', middle-class Negro. I guess I was the first black person in Savannah
to have a zoysia lawn.   HOSEA WILLIAMS

Modern-day white Southerners would say, on those infrequent occasions when the subject was raised, that they did not believe they were accountable for the sins of their grandfathers. But I know few who would not admit, in the darkest and most secret chambers of their souls, and perhaps best after an evening of bourbon in some summer-evening Atlanta backyard, that they were accountable; that they did share some of the blame; that they did bear the burden throughout their lives; and that they knew of no effective way to relieve themselves of this burden.

FRED POWLEDGE

In the South the pattern of segregation is written into the laws. In the North they're not written into the laws and segregation can be more subtle and just as effective. The Negro in the North doesn't know what to expect—he doesn't know where he's going to be admitted or where he's going to be refused. In some ways he is more sure of himself in the South, which may be a negative virtue, but it always helps to know where you stand.

HOKE NORRIS

I've always respected the Southern white man beyond the Northern white man. The Southern white man has always been more honest about segregation than the

Northern white man. The Northern white man claimed the barriers were down, but they were very much up. But the Southern white man let you know in no uncertain terms, "Nigger, I don't want you eatin' in my business." And I've always felt that the Southern white man was much more religious. When he says something, he means it more. So when he tells ya, "You can come on in now," he's 'bout not joking. He pretty much means that you can come on in.

MARTIN LUTHER KING, JR.

I know Negroes who prefer the South and white Southerners, because "at least there you don't have to play any guessing games!" The guessing games referred to have driven more than one Negro into the narcotics ward, the madhouse, or the river.

JAMES BALDWIN

There are few spectacles more devilishly perplexing to a sophisticated, knowledgeable Northern white than witnessing a meeting between a Southern white and a Southern black, perfect strangers to one another, and listening as they spring, almost immediately after discovering their shared origins, into a discussion of "home" or "down home," or sometimes just "back

there,'' in a language that the Northerner can hardly
begin to comprehend.   FRED POWLEDGE

When a black man and a white man meet, neither
man knows where the other one is located in the
journey against prejudice. But when the two men realize that each has made that journey, then there's a
real bond. And that bond is stronger in the South than
you'll find anywhere else in the country.

AL GORE

We went across the South on Super Tuesday without a
single catcall or boo, without a single ugly sign. Not
until we got to New York and the North did the lit-
mus tests of race and religion spout from the mouths
of public officials.   JESSE JACKSON

For the black man, there's no difference between the
North and the South. In the South they don't mind
how close I get as long as I don't get too big; in the
North they don't mind how big I get as long as I
don't get too close.   DICK GREGORY

CIVIL RIGHTS

I had felt for a long time that if I was ever told to get up so a white person could sit, that I would refuse to do so.   ROSA PARKS

I've never said I was against integration. It should have started right after the Civil War. But why single out the South? The South has been imposed on long enough. It's the orphan of the nation.

MARTHA MITCHELL

In the name of the greatest people that have ever trod the earth, I draw the line in the dust and toss the gauntlet before the feet of tyranny, and I say: ''Segregation now—segregation tomorrow—segregation forever.''   GEORGE WALLACE

The prevailing mood is escapist; actuality is not yet at hand, and most Southerners still hope that it will go away.

HARRY S. ASHMORE, on the move
to desegregate the public schools, 1956

I think someone quoted me as saying six days in Jefferson County Jail would be more educational to these children than six months in the segregated Birmingham schools that they were attending.

WYATT TEE WALKER, former executive director of the Southern Christian Leadership Conference, on the decision to involve children in the Birmingham marches of 1961

I'm taking a ride on the Greyhound bus line,
I'm a-riding the front seat to Jackson this time.
Hallelujah, I'm a-travelin',
Hallelujah, ain't it fine?
Hallelujah, I'm a-travelin'
Down Freedom's main line.
SONG OF THE 1961 FREEDOM RIDES

What they propose . . . [is] something beyond secession from the Union. What they urge is secession from civilization.

JONATHAN DANIELS, on roadblocks thrown up against desegregation

One of the reasons that Ole Miss was such a difficult university to desegregate was the emphasis that the

Mississippi press gave to the desegregation of Mississippi.   MYRLIE EVERS

People in Mississippi had a very strong emotional re-
sponse to Meredith. It was just Mississippi and Ole
Miss against the world.
                    JAN ROBERTSON, managing editor of the
                              Ole Miss student newspaper

Governor Barnett was intransigent and he was also
stupid. He had a narrow political vision. He knew
that Meredith was going to the University of Mississippi, he just didn't want it to be his fault.
                    BURKE MARSHALL, assistant attorney general
                         for civil rights under President Kennedy

What really happened in the Meredith case when the
state decided to resist was that they were playing out
the last chapter of the Civil War.
                    CONSTANCE BAKER MOTLEY, NAACP attorney
                            who represented James Meredith

The situation was as close as you could get to an
irreconcilable difference between the North and the

South. There'd been nothing like it since the Civil War.

> HERBERT BROWNELL, President Eisenhower's
> attorney general during the Little Rock
> public school integration crisis

Faubus was not a lawyer; he was not much of a businessman, he had nothing to fall back on other than to be governor. . . . Somebody told him, "If you can whip up this thing and holler 'nigger' loud enough, you can be elected for a third term."

> WILEY BRANTON, NAACP lawyer who filed
> suit to speed public school integration

Perhaps the most charitable thing that could be said of the Arkansas governor was that he had misunderstood the past, miscalculated the present, and ignored the future.

> HARRY S. ASHMORE on Orval Faubus, 1957

Can the man howling in the mob imagine General R. E. Lee, CSA, shaking hands with Orval Faubus, governor of Arkansas?   ROBERT PENN WARREN

Once the fight is decisively lost (the verdict has to be decisive), once the Negro has secured the right to vote, has gained admittance to a public library, has fought his way into a desegregated public school, has been permitted to sup at a lunch counter, the typical white Southerner will shrug his shoulders, resume his stride, and go on. He has, after all, shared a land with his black neighbors for a long while. . . . There is now one less fight which history requires of him. He has done his ancestral duty. He . . . can relax a bit more.   LESLIE DUNBAR

There is a theory, partly valid, that one reason racism in other parts of America was so late in being discovered was because our racists were more colorful than anybody else's racists.   PAUL HEMPHILL

Ku Klux Klan

My great-grandfather . . . was the first black political candidate in the state of Mississippi. He ran for the border and made it. And the reason he ran for the border, he said, was that the people were very clannish. He didn't mind them having hang-ups, he just didn't want to be one of their hang-ups.

REDD FOXX

I had joined the Klan because of those robes. They made good copy, you know. Good pictures. But after a while, all those guys with the green teeth, they got to me. So I started my own organization, the National Association for the Advancement of White People. We don't have any record of violence. It's the perfect foil for me.   DAVID DUKE

We had to get David out of the Klan. He was seducing all the wives.   KU KLUX KLAN MEMBER, 1986

Whether they like it or not, every political rabble-rouser is the godfather of these cross burnings and dynamiters who sneak about and give a bad name to the South.   WILLIAM HARTSFIELD

It is a harvest, too, for those so-called Christian ministers who have chosen to preach hate instead of compassion. Let them now find pious words and raise their hands in deploring the bombing of a synagogue.

You do not preach and encourage hate for the Negro and hope to restrict it to that field.

> RALPH MCGILL, in a Pulitzer Prize-winning editorial on the bombing of an Atlanta synagogue

As a Southerner, it makes me feel angry when I see them [the Ku Klux Klan] with a Confederate battle flag, because I remember Judah P. Benjamin, who was secretary of state, he was a Jew. And I remember General Pat Cleburne of Arkansas, who died in battle not far from this very spot, and General Beauregard of Louisiana—brave men. Both were Catholics. . . . And sometimes when I see the raising of a cross, I remember that the One who was crucified taught us to have faith, to hope, and not to hate but to love one another.   JIMMY CARTER

POLITICS

The demagogues have always understood that Southerners love the grand gesture.   ALAN LEVERITT

For many years the candidates with the best chance to win public office in the South were the men who had lost an arm or a leg in the Civil War. The lost-limb tradition continued in Southern politics far beyond the time that the loss was associated with ''wounds of battle.'' Finally it made no difference how you lost the leg or the arm, you had the best chance of winning public office.   HARRY GOLDEN

I am an Alabama Democrat, not a national Democrat. I'm not kin to those folks. The difference between a national Democrat and an Alabama Democrat is like the difference between a Communist and a non-Communist.   GEORGE WALLACE

George Wallace is dishing out his politics the way many of his fellow Alabamians like their whiskey and religion—as hot and raw as white lightnin' and as primitive as Baptist fundamentalism.

JAMES R. DICKINSON

The southern Democrats are in the saddle and the northern Democrats must tag along as best they may, no matter what ill may betide.

REPRESENTATIVE JOHN JACOB ROGERS, 1913

Most of the other Southern states have had their share of goons in the state Capitol, but Georgia seems to work at it harder.   PAUL HEMPHILL

Only this country can afford a Lester. We need him for levity. The longer you look at him, the funnier it is. It's funny that he got elected, and it's funny the state didn't crumble.

BOB COHEN, on Governor Lester Maddox

Race permeates Southern politics like the twilight mist hanging in the marshlands that slither with the sounds of night creatures. It is always just below the surface of every public utterance, a chorus of whispers in the clatter of elective politics.   ELI EVANS

It would not have mattered if Senator Goldwater had advocated the collectivization of the plantations and open saloons in Jackson; he voted against the Civil Rights bill, and that was that.

WALKER PERCY, on why Goldwater carried
five southern states in the 1964 presidential
election

Every Southerner, every white Southern politician has been freed by the '64 and '65 Civil Rights acts.

NICHOLAS KATZENBACH, attorney general under President Lyndon Johnson

The Voting Rights Act did not just guarantee the vote for black people. It liberated the South, both black and white. JIMMY CARTER

JIMMY CARTER

The first symbolic event in the mythology of the contemporary South was the election of Jimmy Carter in 1976. STEPHEN A. SMITH

Ol' Southern boys around the world . . . lurched to their collective feet, spilling right smart amounts of bourbon and branch water over the rims of their gold goblets or jelly glasses, and with wet eyes huskily proclaimed: "We ain't trash no more."

LARRY L. KING, on the election of Jimmy Carter as President

He symbolized the modern South—desegregated, upwardly mobile, more cosmopolitan in its politics, a champion of agribusiness, well educated, adroit in public imagery. WILLIAM COOPER and THOMAS TERRILL

Thanks to Jimmy Carter, the journalistic trendsetters and social scientists have discovered the South. They are now going to explain the Southerner to himself and leave the ethnic in peace. MIKE ROYKO

GEORGIA

I am determined that at the end of this administration we shall be able to stand up anywhere in the world

—in New York, California, or Florida—and say "I'm a Georgian," and be proud of it.

JIMMY CARTER, Inaugural Address as
Georgia governor, 1971

The average Georgian votes the Democratic ticket, attends the Baptist or Methodist church, goes home to midday dinner, relies greatly on high cotton prices, and is so good a family man that he flings wide his doors to even the most distant of his wife's cousins' cousins.   FEDERAL WRITERS' PROJECT, *Georgia: A Guide to Its Towns and Countryside*

I am in a great big rambling, shambling village which they call a city here.

WILLIAM MAKEPEACE THACKERAY
on Macon, Georgia

Albany was one of those areas where blacks seemed to be still intact culturally. The singing, the folklore, had a kind of indigenous power to it that meant you couldn't walk away from Albany, Georgia.

ANDREW YOUNG

Savannah is a living tomb about which there still clings a sensuous aura as in old Corinth.   HENRY MILLER

Savannah: The name begins with a whisper and ends with a sigh, inciting dreams of a never-never South, of belles and balls, soft accents and gentle courtesy, of magnolias and Spanish moss, and all the rest.
ANTHONY WOLFF

In the spring, when the yellow forsythia gives way to the blue wisteria, which gives way to the dogwood, dazzling white. Then the citizens [of Savannah] feel the urge to inhale May.   CHARLES KURALT

Savannah, Georgia, is the most integrated city south of the Mason-Dixon line.   MARTIN LUTHER KING, JR.

ATLANTA

If anything good spills over into the South, it comes from Atlanta.   HELEN BULLARD

Atlanta is the only city I know where everyone speaks openly, and often fondly, of "the power structure."

TAYLOR BRANCH

When many other southern cities put dogs and cattle prods, fire hoses in the streets, Atlanta in the sixties went to the bargaining table. It's called the Atlanta style. MAYNARD JACKSON

By the conclusion of *Gone with the Wind,* the only attitude of Scarlett that remains unreconstructed is her attitude toward blacks. . . . Yet, it's easy to predict that Scarlett's keen nose for a dollar would have eventually led her to change her ways. Of all people, she would have seen what Atlanta's white fathers recognized in the 1960s: Segregation was the worst stumbling block to growth. After all, Atlanta was not a city too enlightened to hate, but too busy.

STEVE ONEY

From the Potomac to Mobile Bay, from Hatteras to the Rio Grande, there is no God but Advertising, and Atlanta is his prophet.

GERALD W. JOHNSON, 1923

Every time I look at Atlanta I see what a quarter of a million Confederate soldiers died to prevent.

JOHN SHELTON REED

Atlanta is an upstart. A lusty country lass has come late to town, with lace on her parasol and red clay on her petticoats. Wise, now, in the ways of the world; a rich girl, a sophisticated lady wheeling and dealing and playing with the world's great and near great, who come courting in endless streams. But a hoyden, for all that.   ANNE RIVERS SIDDONS

The new Atlanta, sprung from the ashes of the old, is a hideous, nondescript city combining the evil, ugly traits of both North and South.   HENRY MILLER

I heard it said that the "architecture" of Atlanta is rococola. The pun is bad, but what the city would be like without Coca-Cola is hard to conceive.

JOHN GUNTHER, 1947

Coca-Cola's home is in Atlanta, and if we wanted to say "Co-Coler," we could.   LEWIS GRIZZARD

You can go to any gathering of businessmen in Atlanta, and I'll bet you five dollars to a ginger cake that at least 50 percent of them will not be natives.

EDWARD D. SMITH, chairman of Atlanta's
First National Bank, 1974

In that day Georgians invariably put the state's name after the town when they told you where they were from—"Valdosta, Georgia," or "Rossville, Georgia"—and then almost always added how many miles it was from Atlanta.   CELESTINE SIBLEY

Everybody in the state of Georgia knew the phrase "them lyin' Atlanta newspapers." It was first introduced by Georgia governor Eugene Talmadge in the thirties. Whenever the papers would criticize him, he would go to South Georgia somewhere and talk about "them lyin' Atlanta newspapers."   LEWIS GRIZZARD

FLORIDA

Physically and socially, Florida has its own North and South, but its northern area is strictly Southern and its southern area definitely Northern.

FEDERAL WRITERS' PROJECT, *Florida: A Guide to the Southernmost State*

From north to south, this was the view: first, the low-rolling, pine-covered hills of the north and panhandle, close kin to the red clay hills of neighboring Georgia and Alabama, a land of magnolias and the languid Suwanee River, live oaks and Spanish moss.

NEAL R. PEIRCE

I just got wonderful news from my real estate agent in Florida: They found land on my property.

MILTON BERLE

In none of the forty-eight states does life leap so suddenly, in an hour's motor drive, from the suburban snooze to the primeval ooze.   ALISTAIR COOKE

I am stopping for two or three days at the "oldest city in America"—two or three being none too much to sit in wonderment at the success with which it has outlived its age.   HENRY JAMES on St. Augustine

An orange grown in Florida usually has a thin and tightly fitting skin, and is also heavy with juice. Californians say that if you want to eat a Florida orange you have to get into a bathtub first. In Florida, it is said that you can run over a California orange with a ten-ton truck and not even wet the pavement.

JOHN McPHEE

Palm Beach is human nature at its lowest form. The wealthy people here are bored, with nothing to do. They hate to see people who are happy.

ROXANNE PULITZER

An example of what God would do if he had money.

RONALD HASTINGS, on Palm Beach

Miami Beach is where neon goes to die.

LENNY BRUCE

Miami is more American than America.

GARRY WILLS

WASHINGTON, D.C.

A city of Southern efficiency and Northern charm.

JOHN F. KENNEDY

There are a number of things wrong with Washington. One of them is that everyone has been too long away from home. DWIGHT D. EISENHOWER

That Indian swamp in the wilderness.

THOMAS JEFFERSON

Washington isn't a city, it's an abstraction.

DYLAN THOMAS

Has the Southern heritage become an old hunting jacket that one slips on comfortable while at home but discards when he ventures abroad in favor of some more conventional or modish garb? Or is it perhaps an attic full of ancestral wardrobes useful only in connection with costume balls and play-acting—staged primarily in Washington, D.C.?

C. VANN WOODWARD

The pretentions of Washington are often redeemed by a small-town, even a country feeling.

JAN MORRIS

Washington combines the worst features of North and South; here is neither the paternalism of Atlanta or Tuscaloosa nor the relative freedom of Chicago and New York. Negroes who have lived in many parts of the country say that nowhere else in America is there such bitter mutual race hatred.

ALDEN STEVENS, 1947

MARYLAND

[Maryland is] the northernmost outpost of the Old Confederacy in the geographical sense, but spiritually of its deepest heart. JAMES M. CAIN

It is more like an English town than most of its trans-
atlantic brethren, and the ways of its inhabitants are
English. . . . The country looks as hunting country
should look, whereas no man that ever crossed a field
after a pack of hounds would feel the slightest wish
to attempt that process in New England or New York.

ANTHONY TROLLOPE on Baltimore

MᵢₛₛₒURᵢ

A Missourian gets used to Southerners thinking him a
Yankee, a Northerner considering him a cracker, a
Westerner sneering at his effete Easternness, and the
Easterner taking him for a cowhand.

WILLIAM LEAST HEAT MOON

This state is a mélange of peoples, occupations, and
resources. It would be difficult to pinpoint it, except
to say that, in general, it is Southern.

PEARL BUCK

Missouri is the abolitionist North with its belief in
equal rights for all men and women. It is the plan-

tation South with its old ideas of a leisure society. It is the industrial East, busy, noisy, mechanical, commercial. It is the grazing West, miles and miles of pasture and prize livestock in every direction.

IRVING DILLIARD

SOUTH CAROLINA

South Carolinians are Sandlappers—another word for clayeaters. Once a term of derision, the Sandlappers tag now is a badge of honor.   ROY WILDER, JR.

No Southern state can match South Carolina's ability to resist the claims of black people without becoming the object of national scorn.   ROBERT COLES

Charleston sums up this tragedy of the South. It is a lovely city, warm and graceful; but over it hangs a pall of obsession, distorting thoughts and perverting motives, turning almost every conversation into a rude clash of prejudices.   JAMES MORRIS

If there is a finer place than Charleston in the spring, when azaleas bloom in every garden behind every wrought-iron gate on every winding street, I don't know it.   CHARLES KURALT

The historic Charleston district is no roped-off stage-set enclave; it is downtown, and it is alive.

NEAL R. PEIRCE

Charleston is a beautiful memory, a corpse whose lower limbs have been resuscitated.

HENRY MILLER

The manners of the inhabitants of Charleston are as different from those of the other North American cities as are the products of their soil. . . . There prevails here a finer manner of life, and on the whole there are more evidences of courtesy than in the northern cities.   JOHANN DAVID SCHOEPF

There are, I am fairly sure, more pancake houses per capita in Myrtle Beach than anyplace else on the East Coast.   FRED POWLEDGE

It's funny what grown-ups do if you ask them if they ever cruised Myrtle Beach. . . . They lean back in their office chairs and open up. They tell you something like, if you grew up in South Carolina, cruising Ocean Boulevard is tantamount to a good Christian being baptized. It's a must. Something you just have to do. SALLEY MCINERNEY

South Carolinians are among the rare folk in the South who have no secret envy of Virginians.
FEDERAL WRITERS' PROJECT, *South Carolina: A Guide to the Palmetto State*

Before a Virginian, a North Carolinian is supposed to stand cap in hand. And faced with hauteur of an old family of Charleston, South Carolina, even a Virginian may shuffle his feet and look uneasy.
RICHARD WEAVER

NORTH CAROLINA

North Carolina has been referred to as "The valley of humility between two mountains of conceit." [Virginia and South Carolina].   HARRY GOLDEN

North Carolina begins with the brightness of sea sands and ends with the loneliness of the Smokies reaching in chill and cloud to the sky.

OVID WILLIAM PIERCE

It is winter on the Outer Banks. At this time of year you can walk nearly a hundred miles down the wild barrier beaches without meeting another living soul. Hunch your back against the wind, put your hands in your pockets, and ponder, as you walk, the mystery of the first Europeans to know this coast.

CHARLES KURALT

There's something very fascinating about the towns and cities of eastern North Carolina. They have retained much of their original character, refusing to break their long-cherished continuity with the past. . . .

Most of these old Anglo-Saxon communities can trace their earliest beginnings to a single Englishman who had been given a large land grant from the king.

HARRY GOLDEN

North Carolinians are Tar Heels (two words) and were once known as Tar Boilers, both nicknames pertaining to the state's early prominence in the naval stores industry. ROY WILDER, JR.

In Johnston County, North Carolina, you can't be any kind of a farmer at all without a mule.

AVA GARDNER

I suppose Asheville is again overrun with pretty girls. They're all right if you can just look at them without having to talk to them, but when they open their mouths, all is lost. I am convinced that the average girl around Asheville (aged twenty or over) has the brain capacity of a fourteen-year-old child.

THOMAS WOLFE

Only one good thing can come of this. The monkeys in the jungle will be pleased to know that the North

Carolina legislature has absolved them of any responsibility for humanity in general and the North Carolina legislature in particular.

> SAM ERVIN, speaking against the proposed
> ban on teaching evolution

I think it proves that North Carolina doesn't want a senator who knows how to cuss.

> BOB THOMAS, on losing the Democratic
> senatorial primary, 1990

I've never yet been in a state . . . where there is as much state pride as North Carolinians feel about North Carolina. RICHARD ADLER

VIRGINIA

I love Virginians because Virginians are all such snobs and I like snobs. A snob has to spend so much time being a snob that he has little time left to meddle with you. WILLIAM FAULKNER

Virginia, where charm is laid on so thick you could saw it off in chunks and export it.

WILLIAM GOLDING

Jefferson pronounced it the finest scenery he had ever seen—but he was a Virginian.

FREDERICK LAW OLMSTED, on Harpers Ferry (then in Virginia)

Our society is neither scientific nor splendid, but independent, hospitable, correct, and neighborly.

THOMAS JEFFERSON

They say you should never let a Virginian start talking about his family because you're liable never to shut him up.

EARL HAMNER

All eastern Virginians are Shintoists under the skin. Genealogy makes history personal to them in terms of family. Kinship to the eighth degree usually is recognized. . . . A pleasant society it is, one that does not adventure rashly into new acquaintances but welcomes with a certain stateliness of manner those who come with letters from friends.

DOUGLAS SOUTHALL FREEMAN

The Virginian idea, it must be clearly understood, was not what is today called the American dream. The Virginian did not dream of a democracy, with its literal meaning of the rule of the people. His dream was to found an aristocratic republic, in which superior individuals would emerge to rule the many.

CLIFFORD DOWDEY

The essential antagonism of Virginia and New England was afterwards to become, and to remain, an element of the first influence in American history. Each might have learned much from the other, but neither did so till, at last, the strife of their contending principles shook the continent.

FRANCIS PARKMAN

Next to brandy, next to card-playing, next to horse-racing, the thing that has done Virginia more harm than any other in the course of her past history has been her insatiable appetite for federal politics.

HENRY ALEXANDER WISE,
Virginia Governor, 1855

You Episcopalians may have made most of the history and all the mint juleps in Virginia, but you have left

your politics and your laws to the Methodists and
Baptists.   ELLEN GLASGOW

Norfolk is a dirty, low, ill-arranged town, nearly divided by a morass. It has a single creditable public
building, a number of fine private residences, and the
polite society is reputed to be agreeable, refined, and
cultivated, receiving a character from the residing naval officers.   FREDERICK LAW OLMSTED, 1856

Richmond is my home, and a letter to that City will
always reach me in whatever part of the world I may
be.   EDGAR ALLAN POE

Broad streeted Richmond . . .
The trees in the streets are old trees used to living with
*   people.*
Family trees that remember your grandfather's name.
                          STEPHEN VINCENT BENÉT

KENTUCKY

Kentuckians have ever been trying to make up for not being born Virginians. They have seized on their special claim to bourbon whiskey as giving them the right to arrogate the mint julep to themselves.

RICHARD BARKSDALE HARWELL

I returned home to my family with a determination to bring them as soon as possible to live in Kentucke, which I esteemed a second paradise.

DANIEL BOONE, 1784

Great tall, raw-boned Kentuckians, attired in hunting shirts, and trailing their loose joints over a vast extent of territory, with the easy lounge peculiar to the race.

HARRIET BEECHER STOWE

I have witnessed a strange thing—a Kentucky election—and I am disposed to give you an account of it. An election in Kentucky lasts three days, and during that period whiskey and apple toddy flow through

our cities and villages like the Euphrates through an-
cient Babylon.

GEORGE D. PRENTISS, in a letter to
a New England newspaper, 1830

A dashing Kentuckian intimates to you the richness of
the soil; saying, "If you plant a nail at night, 'twill
come up a spike next morning."

HARRIET MARTINEAU

Depending on which Kentuckian you ask, the 114-
year-old Kentucky Derby may be defined as anything
from an experience that is arguably better than sex to
a quasi-religious awakening.

MARTHA HUME

Frankfort is the capital of Kentucky, and is as quietly
dull a lit-tle town as I ever visited. . . . The legislature
of the state was not sitting when I was there and the
grass was growing in the streets.

ANTHONY TROLLOPE

A good many Northerners terminated their river jour-
neys at Louisville—which accounts for the fact that

the town still casts a lusty if not majority Republican vote.   A. B. GUTHRIE

The city is not definitely Northern or Southern, Eastern or Western, and it may be that its residents are thus spared the emotional necessity of being representatives of a region whether they want to be or not.

FRED POWLEDGE, on Louisville

Louisville quickly became a part of the heartthrob of material America. It left the lavish rural hospitality, traditions, and the nostalgia to Lexington while it eyed the future.   THOMAS D. CLARK

Should you come to Lexington, leave your best thoughts behind. The theories you have most resolved, the results that are to you most certain, pack them close away, and give them no airing here. Your mind must stifle, if your body thrives.

FREDERICK LAW OLMSTED

ARKANSAS

An intriguing mix of geography and culture—Southern, Western, and Midwestern at the same time—Arkansas can seem like an extension of Texas at Texarkana and of Mississippi at Helena.

PETER APPLEBOME

Arkansas had a reputation in the nineteenth century of being a place of renegades that was so dangerous and crazy no self-respecting person would move there.

JEANIE WHAYNE

If I could rest anywhere it would be in Arkansaw where the men are of the real half-horse, half-alligator breed such as grows nowhere else on the face of the universal earth.   ATTRIBUTED TO DAVY CROCKETT

Arkansas is a great state. It must be, otherwise De-Soto, who discovered about everything there was to be discovered in the Southwest, would have passed it by.   HENRY MILLER

People in Stamps used to say that the whites in our town were so prejudiced that a Negro couldn't buy vanilla ice cream.   MAYA ANGELOU

This the only Southern state which does not have a single statue of a Confederate general in the state-house.   TRISTRAM COFFIN

> *Biggest fool I ever saw*
> *Come from the state of Arkansaw;*
> *Put his shirt on over his coat,*
> *Button his britches up round his throat.*
>   AMERICAN FOLK SONG

I didn't make Arkansas the butt of ridicule. God did.
          H. L. MENCKEN

But wit is so common in Arkansas that it does not distinguish a man—not while he is in Arkansas. It is the tradition of the land.   C. L. EDSON

Little Rock is a city in which "old money" means your father had some, and he got it from his father when it was brand new. The state's truly wealthy, virtually without exception, are self-made. Entrepreneurship is valued all the more for its scarcity.

STEVE BARNES

Without being facetious or anything, Arkansas without chickens would be a damn poor place to be today.

DON TYSON

Like a hotbed of tranquillity.

EDWARD DURRELL STONE's description of his birthplace, Fayetteville, Arkansas

It takes four ingredients—the right seed, the right soil, the right climate, and the know-how. If you've got all that—and then if you grow it right around Hope, Arkansas—you've got yourself a devil of a big watermelon. C. M. "POD" ROGERS

I still believe in a place called Hope.

BILL CLINTON

LOUISIANA

In Louisiana there are stretches of bayou country whose beauty is of a nature such as only the Chinese poets have captured.   HENRY MILLER

Baton Rouge was clothed in flowers like a bride—no, much more so; like a greenhouse. For we were in the absolute South now—no modifications, no compromises, no halfway measures.   MARK TWAIN

They say Louisiana is somewhat like a banana republic, say Guatemala. That's not true. They speak better English in Guatemala.   JACK KNEECE

Over one-quarter of the population of Louisiana still speaks some French, but not with much pride.
                                        CHRISTOPHER HALLOWELL

Anytime you want a Cajun to shut up, just handcuff him.
                    JAMES CARVILLE, on the Cajun habit of
                                        gesturing while talking

This state's full of sapsucker, hillbilly, and Cajun relatives of mine, and there ain't enough dignity in the bunch of 'em to keep a chigger still long enough to brush his hair.   HUEY LONG

The poor people of Louisiana have only three friends: Jesus Christ, Sears and Roebuck, and Earl Long.

EARL LONG

In Louisiana we don't bet on football games. . . . We bet on whether a politician is going to be indicted or not.   MARK DUFFY

People in Louisiana have an ambivalent attitude about corruption. On the one hand, we deplore it. On the other hand, we brag about it.

T. HARRY WILLIAMS

New Orleans

If I had to live in a city, I think I would prefer New Orleans to any other—both Southern and Catholic and with indications that the Devil's existence is freely recognized.   FLANNERY O'CONNOR

My strongest impression of New Orleans is, that while it affords an instructive study, and yields some enjoyment to a stranger, it is the last place in which men are gathered together whereon who prizes his humanity would wish to live.   HARRIET MARTINEAU

Great Babylon is come up before me. Oh, the wickedness, the idolatry of this place. . . . Pray for your sister in a heathen land.

ANDREW JACKSON'S WIFE, RACHEL,
on New Orleans, in a letter

No city perhaps on the globe, in an equal number of human beings, presents a greater contrast of national manners, language, and complexion than does New Orleans. WILLIAM DARBY, 1817

New Orleans might be exotic in some respects but in others it [is] exactly like everyplace else.
A. J. LIEBLING

New Orleans is both intimately related to the South and yet in a real sense cut adrift not only from the South but the rest of Louisiana. . . . Out and over a watery waste and there it is, a proper enough American city and yet within the next few hours the tourist is apt to see more nuns and naked women than he ever saw before. WALKER PERCY

It is a town where an architect, a gourmet, or a roué is in hog heaven.
GEORGE SESSIONS PERRY, on New Orleans, 1947

There is no architecture in New Orleans, except in the cemeteries. MARK TWAIN

No American city has been a more prolific mother to the musical world [than New Orleans], and none has been more neglectful of her progeny. LAWRENCE WRIGHT

Joe Oliver left New Orleans in 1919, Louis Armstrong left in '22 to join him in Chicago. It's been leave, leave, leave ever since. ELLIS MARSALIS

New Orleans in spring-time, just when the orchards were flushing over with peach-blossoms, and the sweet herbs came to flavor the julips—seemed to me the city of the world where you can eat and drink the most and suffer the least.

WILLIAM MAKEPEACE THACKERAY, 1862

But in New Orleans proper, that marvelous confection of sleaziness and peeling paint that only an 88 percent humidity (the annual average) can produce, the primary industry is now tourism.

JOEL GARREAU

New Orleans could wreck your liver and poison your blood. It could destroy you financially. It could shun you or embrace you, teach you tricks of the heart you thought Tennessee Williams was just kidding about. And in August it could break your spirit.

JULIE SMITH

This town [New Orleans] consumes more alcohol than any other place on Earth—because we start earlier. Drinking a Ramoz fizz or a Sazerac with breakfast is considered normal behavior. ELLA BRENNAN

Nowhere is the system of exclusion more finely honed than in New Orleans, where social status parades each year in Mardi Gras, advertising class distinctions more blatantly than in any other city in America.

ELI EVANS

Where more men own white tie and tails than any other city in the world.

LOCAL HABERDASHER on New Orleans

People from outside New Orleans think the Queen of Carnival is competitive and chosen on beauty, charm, and wisdom. But, because of my father, they would have chosen me if I had two heads; and then they would have put a crown on each head and walked around the ball saying, "Isn't she a beautiful two-headed queen!" FORMER COMUS QUEEN

You know, I don't think New Orleans is ever going to change, because I don't think in the scheme of things, it's supposed to change. But I took a lot from this place. I feel good about New Orleans . . . I mean I could finish out my life anywhere—Paris, whatever—and I'd still be what I am. A New Orleanian.

ELLIS MARSALIS

ALABAMA

Alabama, for some reason I cannot determine, seems to me to be the most southern state of the South.

PEARL BUCK

I was born in Alabama, but I only lived there for a month before I'd done everything there was to do.

PAULA POUNDSTONE

Alabama . . . seems to have a bad name even among those who reside in it.   J. S. BUCKINGHAM, 1842

Birmingham has made a lot of progress . . . progress that they just didn't decide to make, but progress that came through agony.   ABRAHAM WOOD

Birmingham is not like the rest of the state. It is an industrial monster sprung up in the midst of a slow-moving pastoral. It does not belong. . . . Birmingham is a new city in an old land.   CARL CARMER

Artis loved his Birmingham with an insatiable passion, from the south side to the north side, in the freezing-cold rainy weather, when the red clay would slide down the sides of hills and run into the streets, and in the lush green summers, when the green kudzu vine covered the sides of the mountains and grew up on trees and telephone poles and the air was heavy and moist with the smell of gardenias and barbecue.
FANNIE FLAGG, *Fried Green Tomatoes at the Whistle Stop Café*

In another five years the old glow of such lovely towns as Tuscaloosa, Athens, Marion, and Eufaula will have vanished, and the Pittsburghs and Newarks of the South will rise in their stead.   SARA HAARDT, 1925

I have never once thought of work in connection with the word "Mobile." Not anybody working. A city surrounded with shells, the empty shells of bygone fiestas. Bunting everywhere, and the friable relics of yesterday's carnival. Gaiety always in retreat, always vanishing, like clouds brushing a mirror. In the very center of this glissando, Mobile itself, very prim, very proper, Southern and not Southern, listless but upright, slatternly yet respectable, bright but not wicked.

HENRY MILLER

The drugstores are bright at night with the organdie balloons of girls' dresses under the big electric fans. Automobiles stand along the curbs in front of open frame houses at dusk, and sounds of supper being prepared drift through the soft splotches of darkness to the young world that moves every evening out of doors. Telephones ring, and the lacy blackness under the trees disgorges young girls in white and pink, leaping over the squares of warm light toward the tinkling sound with an expectancy that people have only in places where any event is a pleasant one.

ZELDA FITZGERALD, on Montgomery

[The source of] the most hidebound political thinking, the most corrupt county government and justice, the most friction and race violence, and much of the drag on the South's general progress.

> RALPH MCGILL, on some of
> Alabama's rural counties

I always felt that Alabama was sort of mean, but Mississippi could be deadly. CLAUDE SITTON

Rural Mississippi and Alabama—for journalists, the bellwether for the region—differ so markedly from the rest of the South that they surely rate special attention, for too long they have distorted the national view of the Southern psyche. ELI EVANS

Mississippi

Northerners, provincials that they are, regard the South as one large Mississippi. Southerners, with their eye for distinction, place Mississippi in a class by itself.

> V. O. KEY, JR.

Greenville [Mississippi] is a place of Southern comfort so compelling, despite its startling pockets of poverty, that people here feel obligated to get along.

SHARON MCKERN

The first thing you have to understand about the Delta is that all the business about moonlight, magnolias, and Anglo-Saxon bloodlines has to go out the window. The Delta is a great melting pot.

SHELBY FOOTE

In a place like Mississippi, people have such intimate knowledge about each other. In some ways it's shocking that they know so much about their parents and grandparents and all the details. BILL FERRIS

If I leave Mississippi . . . it will not be for the reasons of the other sons and daughters of my father. . . . It will be because the pervasive football culture bores me and the proliferating Kentucky Fried Chicken stands appall me, and the neon lights have begun to replace the trees. ALICE WALKER

In truth, as I would come to understand, Mississippi may have been the only state in the Union (or certainly one of a half dozen in the South) which had produced a genuine set of exiles, almost in the European sense: alienated from home yet forever drawn back to it, seeking some form of personal liberty elsewhere yet obsessed with the texture and complexity of the place from which they had departed as few Americans from other states could ever be.

WILLIE MORRIS

I am a Mississippian in all respects—even the bad ones. JAMES MEREDITH

Mississippi begins in the lobby of a Memphis, Tennessee, hotel and extends south to the Gulf of Mexico. It is dotted with little towns concentric about the ghosts of the horses and mules once tethered to the hitchrail enclosing the county courthouse and it might almost be said to have only two directions, north and south, since until a few years ago it was impossible to travel east or west in it unless you walked or rode one of the horses or mules.

WILLIAM FAULKNER, on Mississippi beginning in the Peabody Hotel

TENNESSEE

The Peabody is the Paris Ritz, the Cairo Shepheard's, the London Savoy. . . . If you stand near its fountain in the middle of the lobby, where ducks waddle and turtles drowse, ultimately you will see everybody who is anybody in the Delta.

DAVID COHN, on Memphis's famous hotel

Memphis, always a haven for eccentrics and individualism, is the only locale I know that actually boasts of its craziness.   PETER GURALNICK

Where Philadelphians see Camden, and New Yorkers see Hoboken, Memphians see the Mississippi flood plain, the prettiest green view that can be imagined from a downtown.   DENISE SCOTT BROWN

Stuck inside of Mobile with the Memphis blues again.
BOB DYLAN

Nashville, after all, is Muzak City, U.S.A.
PETER GURALNICK

When I bring in a player, I take him out for a big sparerib dinner, show him Memphis, and take him to my big ol' house overlooking the beautiful Mississippi. Then I ask him, "Boy, do you *really* want to play in Buffalo?"

PEPPER RODGERS, coach of the
Memphis Showboats

"Nashville," the old woman had said, "is a city of schools and churches, whereas Memphis is—well, Memphis is something else again. Memphis is a place of steamboats and cotton gins, of card-playing and hotel society. Anyway," the woman went on to say to Mother, "*you,* my dear Minta, will *love* Memphis."

PETER TAYLOR, *A Summons to Memphis*

The town that calls itself "Music City, U.S.A.," is the place where the music is manufactured, bought, sold, taped, mixed, packaged, and hyped, but not necessarily the place where it may be heard and enjoyed.

FRED POWLEDGE, on Nashville

Other cities might lay claim to being the heart or soul of a certain sound, but only Nashville can proclaim itself the physical embodiment of a style of music. In Nashville, performers' houses are laid open, and their homes become museums.   MICHAEL MCCALL

[It is a city] cleanly divided in half by the Cumberland River. And just as Janus faces two directions, so, too, does Nashville—privation and spirituality to the east, the indulgences of the good life to the west.

JESSE HILL FORD

THE MISSISSIPPI RIVER

It remains what it always was—a kind of huge rope, no matter with what knots and frayings, tying the United States together.   JOHN GUNTHER

The Mississippi is a just and equitable river; it never tumbles one man's farm overboard without building a new farm just like it for that man's neighbor. This keeps down hard feelings.   MARK TWAIN

The Mississippi . . . with its paddleboats, ferries, and hoot owls, is the most haunted river in the world.

CECIL BEATON

What is the Mississippi River? A washed clod in the rainy night, a soft plopping from drooping Missouri banks, a dissolving, a riding of the tide down the eternal waterbed, a contribution to brown foams, a voyaging past endless vales and trees and levees, down along, down along, by Memphis, Greenville, Eudora, Vicksburg, Natchez, Port Allen, and Port Orleans and the Port of the Deltas, by Potash, Venice, and the Night's Great Gulf, and out.

JACK KEROUAC

THE LAY OF THE LAND

Take away the environment of the South and you might as well have New Jersey.   FRED POWLEDGE

[In the South] is centered all that can please or prosper humankind. A perfect climate above a fertile soil, yields to the husbandman every product of the temperate zone. . . . There, are mountains stored with exhaustless treasures; forest, vast and primeval, and rivers that, tumbling or loitering, run wanton to the sea.   HENRY GRADY

Son, don't be fooled by her beauty. She looks pretty and she is. She babbles like gossip and giggles like a girl. If you didn't care for beauty, looking at her way up here, you might be callin' her a piddlin' river. But, son, she ain't. I've seen her come out of the mountains like a wild stallion with logs in his mane. I've seen her take gristmills and grind them up in their own stones. I've seen her tear up bridges and twist steel until it looked like bands for hogsheads.

RALPH MCGILL, on the Chattahoochee River

The Southern coast is different: a land of incalculable biological energy, of incomparable beauty, of romance and love and nature's violence; of mysterious lush islands and serpentine salt marshes.

FRED POWLEDGE

Most surprising is the Louisiana tree parasite—this is a long, dirty, gray veil hanging from all the tree branches, Spanish moss—graceful yet disfiguring, it seems to rob the trees of their essential freshness.

STEPHEN POTTER

The first grand tree development of the "swamps" is the tall and ghostly cypress. It flourished in our semi-tropical climate of the South, being nourished by warmth, water, and the richest possible soil.

T. B. THORPE

The tree's strange "knees" sticking out of the water and the hanging Spanish moss (which old-timers burned in smudge pots to keep the mosquitoes off) gave us the pleasure of their company, not to be encountered widely in the South anymore because cypress fetches so much as a log and air pollution kills the moss.

EDWARD HOAGLAND

The drawback of writing letters from these parts is that the subject is so supremely disagreeable. Over a thousand miles of railroad I have not seen a beautiful prospect—only swamp, sand, pines, wood cabins or villages and negroes reposing here or there—on the Alabama River a view about as mournful as if it were a tributary to the Styx, on the Mississippi the same dreariness on a wider scale.

WILLIAM MAKEPEACE THACKERAY

KUDZU

It's the scourge of the Deep South, and if we didn't know differently, we'd swear it was a secret weapon that had been brought down from up yonder during the "War of Northern Aggression."

MILDRED JORDAN BROOKS

Here in the South, kudzu's not something you ordinarily give a friend. It's a little like giving a pregnant rabbit as a present to the neighbor's children. Kudzu tends to multiply. On summer nights in Georgia, you can actually hear the kudzu growing. In fact, that's usually the only warning you get.

CARD ATTACHED TO A PACKET OF
KUDZU SEEDS sent to prospective
advertisers in *Southern* magazine

In Georgia, the legend says
That you must close your windows
At night to keep it out of the house.
 JAMES DICKEY, from his poem "Kudzu"

Kudzu's root system may hold a hillside tighter than other plants can. Its starchy taproot may be more easily fermented. Its leaves and stems may produce more methane. But native plants have advantages of their own. For starters, natives won't swallow houses or incur lawsuits. JANET HOBSON, in *Science Digest*

THE CLIMATE

Take of London fog 30 parts; malaria 10 parts; gas leaks 20 parts; dewdrops gathered in a brickyard at sunrise 25 parts; odor of honeysuckle 15 parts, Mix. The mixture will give you the approximate conception of a Nashville drizzle. O. HENRY

Tennessee summer days were not made for work; in fact, many a resident had doubted that they were made at all, but that they sprang to life from the cauldrons of hell.   CARL ROWAN

Can you imagine the Scopes trial in an air-conditioned courthouse? The 100-degree heat, the florid-faces and sweating bodies were what made Dayton, Tennessee, seem savage to Mencken and outsiders, nearly as much as the fundamentalism.   FRED HOBSON

Somedays in the summertime in Mississippi, the weather is so hot you can almost see it.   AMZIE MOORE

In the Mississippi Delta there was nothing gentle about nature. It came at you violently, or in a rush; sometimes it was just plain lazy and at others crazy and wild.   WILLIE MORRIS

I had forgotten springtime in the South, the dogwoods and the azaleas and the girls in halter tops in the gallery on the sixteenth hole at Augusta National.

    LEWIS GRIZZARD

Born of dog days necessity and Depression-era affordability, the seersucker suit is, if you will, vernacular fashion at its best: a cool, crisp answer to the South's sticky summers, climate control *cum* haberdashery, fashion and function all rolled into one. A practical idea turned into the staple of romance and style.

ELIZABETH BYRD

AIR CONDITIONING

It was hard to understand how people had made out here before air conditioning and screens. In the days before travel was easy, this kind of heat would have thrown people into themselves, as much as the winters of the Far North are said to throw Scandinavians in on themselves. And perhaps this six-month summer weather, hot rising to hotter, was a factor in the still-visible degeneracy of a section of the local white population.

V. S. NAIPAUL

Shady, open to whatever breezes decided to blow, the porch was an architectual stepchild of the plantation house's sweeping veranda, offering a modicum of relief from the stuffiness which welled up inside even the best ventilated houses. So pervasive was the impact of the air conditioner that homes built after its arrival rarely even have porches.   DAVID DAWSON

General Sherman may have started the process, but General Electric, with its air conditioners, is going to finish it. The South will become little save the happy hunting grounds of the Holiday Inn.

JOEL GARREAU

Can you imagine Faulkner writing *Absalom, Absalom!* under the spell of central air conditioning? One might, indeed, discover a direct relationship between the rise of air conditioning and the decline of the creative fury of the Southern writer.   FRED HOBSON

SOUTHERN TALK

Storytelling and copulation are the two chief forms of amusement in the South. They're inexpensive and easy to procure.   ROBERT PENN WARREN

The South has a long tradition of slow moving, of standing and watching, of having the time—of giving ourselves the time—to sit, on country porches and courthouse Confederate monuments and on green benches in public parks and tell each other stories, gossip, and use words.   JAMES DICKEY

We work hard, of course, but we do it in a different way. We work hard in order not to work. Any time spent on business is more or less wasted, but you have to do it in order to be able to hunt and fish and gossip.
HARPER LEE

The renaissance of storytelling that has been taking place over these past dozen years . . . is a bona fide national—if not, to some degree, worldwide—phenomenon. And there are, to be sure, a host of top-of-the-line tellers from other parts of the United States. But it is a simple fact of life that the very best of the best tend to hail from the South. Everybody knows this. That's all there is to it.

WILLIAM HEDGEPETH

I think the Southerner is a talker by nature, but not only a talker—we are used to an audience. We are used to a listener and that does something to our narrative style, I think. I think you could talk in the Rocky Mountains. You wouldn't get anything back but an echo.　　EUDORA WELTY

If any one eccentricity nourished the Southerner and gives him space to perform and struggle and fight, it is indirection. . . . No discussion, sermon, or quarrel should be telescoped when it can be drawn out all afternoon with endless opportunity for dodging, feinting, and keeping one's position obscured. . . . Indirection is not dishonesty. It is simply a matter of style.

ROY REED

SOUTHERN WRITERS

The South has produced writers as the Dark Ages
produced saints. ALFRED KAZIN

Why has the South produced so many good writers?
Because we got beat. WALKER PERCY

Southern writers seem to be born to sing. They live
in small towns where they hear the most beautiful
balladry, every day, from their own people and from
the black people. MARGUERITE YOUNG

[Grit Lit is] Southern literature that defiantly makes
itself known as Southern. FRED CHAPPELL

What one wonders, and what a lot of people have
asked themselves, is how in the atmosphere of the
First World War or of the twenties, could a sensitive
Southern writer have lived there?

WILLIAM F. BUCKLEY, JR.

Let's sell everything and move South! How we could write!

> MARJORIE KINNAN RAWLINGS, on seeing the
> St. Johns River for the first time

With the war of 1914–1918, the South re-entered the world—but gave a backward glance that gave us the Southern renascence, a literature conscious of the past in the present.   ALLEN TATE, 1945

When I'm asked why Southern writers particularly have a penchant for writing about freaks, I say it's because we are still able to recognize one.

> FLANNERY O'CONNOR

How many of us, the South's writers-to-be of my generation, were blessed in one way or another, if not blessed alike, in not having gone deprived of the King James Version of the Bible. Its cadence entered into our ears and our memories for good. The evidence, or the ghost of it, lingers in all our books.   EUDORA WELTY

Well, you may write like an angel in the South, but unless you can get those northern publishing gears to turn for you, you're not an American writer.

Roy Blount, Jr.

To be published out of the South still counts the most in the South. Louis D. Rubin, Jr.

One reason many of our poets feel free to be Southern, rather than simply American, is that they are not competing with predecessors of towering reputations as Southern novelists are. Guy Owen

In the South there are more amateur authors than there are rivers and streams. It's not an activity that waits upon talent. In almost every hamlet you'll find at least one lady writing epics in Negro dialect and probably two or three old gentlemen who have impossible historical novels on the way. The woods are full of regional writers, and it is the great horror of every serious Southern writer that he will become one of them. Flannery O'Connor

WILLIAM FAULKNER

So often I'm asked how I could have written a word with William Faulkner living in Mississippi, and this question amazes me. It was like living near a big mountain, something majestic—it made me happy to know it was there, all that work of his life. But it wasn't a helping or hindering presence. Its magnitude, all by itself, made it something remote in my own working life. When I thought of Faulkner it was when I read.   EUDORA WELTY

At his best he penetrated the magnolia curtain of Southern illusions to the secret springs of motive and action. He said, in effect, "This is the way it feels to be Southern"—something the North needs to know and the South may even need to be reminded of.

HORACE JUDSON

Perhaps it's just true that Faulkner, if he had been born in, say, Pasadena, might very well still have had that universal quality of mind, but instead of writing

Light in August he would have gone into television or written universal ads for Jantzen bathing suits.

WILLIAM STYRON

The presence alone of Faulkner in our midst makes a great difference in what the writer can and cannot permit himself to do. Nobody wants his mule and wagon stalled on the same track the *Dixie Limited* is roaring down. FLANNERY O'CONNOR

If this man is a good writer, shrimps whistle "Dixie."

CALDER WILLINGHAM

Trying to send up Faulkner is like trying to do an impression of Little Richard. You had better be able to cut loose. ROY BLOUNT, JR.

I have heard people ask where William Faulkner gets that stuff that goes into his novels—whether he dreams it in nightmares and so on. No one who had spent any time in Mississippi with his ears open would have to ask that question. RICHARD WEAVER

LITERACY & CULTURE

The South don't care a d———n for literature or art. Your best neighbour & kindred never think to buy books. They will borrow from you and beg, but the same man who will always have his wine, has no idea of a library.   WILLIAM GILMORE SIMMS, 1847

Alas for the South! Her books have grown fewer—
She never was much given to literature.
                                J. GORDON COOGLER

George C. Cable believed that Southerners never developed the habit of reading because the weather was too hot.   FRED HOBSON

For all its size and all its wealth and all the "progress" it [the South] babbles of, it is almost as sterile, artistically, intellectually, culturally, as the Sahara Desert.
                                H. L. MENCKEN

You think I don't have culture just because I'm from down in Georgia. Believe me, we got culture there.

We've always had sushi. We just used to call it "bait."   CONGRESSMAN BEN JONES

I spoke at the long-haired college of Harvard; I told them we got people in Alabama as intelligent and refined and cultured as you are and don't you ever forget it. I made the best speech they ever heard up at Harvard and, you know, the next day hundreds of them got their hair cut.   GEORGE WALLACE

RELIGION

If you scratch a Southern teacher, a preacher will wince.   JOHN ANDREW RICE

When the Southern Baptists gathered in general convention each year, they would engage in spectacular public feats of conscience-wrestling, all of which, no matter how vapid the outcome, involved some of the most magnificent exercises of oratory still to be heard in the age, declamations and soliloquies luxurious with

irony, wryness, urgency, indignation. Even their be-
wilderment was uttered on a scale of grandeur.

MARSHALL FRADY

The poor whites and blacks of the rural South were
particularly susceptible to the sensuousness of heart-
pounding old-time religion, there being little else to
bring them hope in those days, and soon the circuit-
riding Southern evangelist became a raw piece of
Americana.   PAUL HEMPHILL

To small children, though, the idea of praising God
in a tent was confusing to say the least. It seemed
somehow blasphemous. The lights hanging overhead,
the soft ground underneath, and the canvas wall that
faintly blew in and out, like cheeks puffed with air,
made for the feeling of a country fair.

MAYA ANGELOU

The Southern Jesus still walks among us, capable of
miracles: curing the sick and making the lame to walk
and the blind to see; a haunting, righteous figure,
stern and straight-backed, ever present and vigilant,

able to mete out instant justice for bad acts and keep
accurate count of the good for the moment.

ELI EVANS

In a word, the Southerner reveres original creation.
His willingness to accept some conditions that his
more energetic Northern cousin will not put up with
is not purely temperamental or climatic; it is religious
or philosophical insofar as it stems from this world-
view. RICHARD WEAVER

It is in a churchy society that most Southerners are
brought up, and it is what they mention in every other
word in their conversation. In a small town like Banner,
if the Baptists couldn't be against the Methodists, they'd
have nothing to talk about. EUDORA WELTY

I'm glad to see so many of my fine Catholic friends
here—they have been so kind to me I sometimes say
I consider myself 40 percent Catholic and 60 percent
Baptist. But I'm in favor of *every* religion with the
possible exception of snake-chucking. Anybody that so
presumes on how he stands on providence that he will

let a snake bite him, I say he deserves what he's got coming to him.

EARL LONG, during a gubernatorial campaign

A lifetime of looking down on the Bible Belt South as only a Virginian can had driven Granny into a bizarre form of heresy: Christianity reminded her of places like Georgia.   FLORENCE KING

In the Old South, the religion of the upper levels of society—typically the church of the planters—was prevailingly secular and social. The planters took their theology for granted; they simply didn't think too much about it.   CLEANTH BROOKS

Back then when there was a death or some tragedy, you used to say to your neighbor, "I'll be praying for you." Today we tell them, "I'll be thinking about you." Something has been lost, and the fundamentalists know it.   WILL CAMPBELL

I'm generalizing here, but in the South the emphasis seems to be on praising Jesus, not obeying Jesus. In

South Georgia people act like the First Commandment is, "Thou shalt go to church," and the Second Commandment is, "Thou shalt get others to go to church."

MILLARD FULLER

I saw a lot of people that I thought were hypocrites in the very religious atmosphere that I grew up in, saying one thing and doing another. But it is a very important part of my life. I think I feel somewhat more comfortable speaking in the rhythms of my faith in my speeches when I'm home in the South than I do in other places.

BILL CLINTON

The South may be described as the Bible Belt in the same offhand and derisive way that the Eastern Seaboard can be identified as the Barbiturate Belt, the roaring raw cities of the Midwest the Tommy-Gun Belt, and the West Coast the Divorce Belt.

HODDING CARTER II, 1950

Professionally it's a nicer life here. It's the Bible Belt, and the clergy has a higher standing.

ELI EVANS, quoting a Conservative rabbi

There is a touching naïveté in the small-town Southerner's respect for the Jewishness of the Jew in his community. It springs from the Southern Protestant's own attachment to biblical Judaism, which is manifested in the basic tenets of the several denominations.

HARRY GOLDEN

I am not certain what it means to be both a Jew and a Southerner—to have inherited the Jewish longing for a homeland while being raised with the Southerner's sense of home.

ELI EVANS

I was a rustic from the Southern provinces who had eaten more barbecued pork than Paschal lamb, who'd spent more time listening to yodels and Delta blues than davening over the Torah.

STEVE STERN

SPORTS

In the East, college football is a cultural attraction. On the West Coast, it is a tourist attraction. In the

Midwest, it is cannibalism. But in the South, it is religion.

> MARINO CASEM, Alcorn State
> University football coach

They like football in this country, but in the South even football is a folk ritual touching on religiosity, and Saturday is a holy day.   WILLIE MORRIS

In Alabama, Coach Bryant is second only to God. We believe that on the eighth day the Lord created the Crimson Tide.   SENATOR JEREMIAH DENTON

I was once surrounded in a Birmingham hotel lobby by a swarm of drunks in red hats and miracle-fiber suits who were saying ''Roll Tide'' to one another. (''Roll Tide'' is what fans of the Alabama Crimson Tide say the way other people say ''What it is?'' or ''Shalom.'') And I didn't like it.

> ROY BLOUNT, JR.

Hell, at Alabama my junior year, when we lost two games, the word was: Rebuild.   JOE NAMATH

[In Alabama] football is less a way out than a way of life. No other sport has a chance in Alabama. In a lot of towns, a kid's father hangs his head in shame if the boy doesn't make the high school team.

PAUL HEMPHILL

White planters who are football fanatics and good old boys from the Class of '57 cheer wildly for black athletes on Saturday afternoon, and as a result of that behavior they find it more difficult to maintain the prejudice on Monday morning.   STEPHEN A. SMITH

I know why we lost the Civil War. We must have had the same officials.

BUM PHILLIPS, on his South team's loss in the Senior Bowl

I like the South because it is so much warmer on the sidelines than it is up North.   TOM LANDRY

Nothing in Atlanta is going to cause much excitement sportswise unless it's drug-related. They are more concerned with Georgia peaches or football than they are about the Braves.

GARY MATHEWS, Braves' outfielder

Fans out here say there are only two seasons: fall football and spring football.

STEVE STONE, Braves' pitcher,
on Atlanta fans, 1986

The black players eventually put Mobile on the baseball map, but we weren't the only ones who took the game to heart. In fact, Mobile was one of the few places in the Deep South—maybe the only place— where baseball wasn't completely overshadowed by football. HANK AARON

The South served the same function in baseball that it served in the nation's economy: It was a colony producing the raw materials—Cobb, Dean, Mays, Aaron—to be shipped North.   FRED HOBSON

Well, they're Southern people, and if they know you are working at home they think nothing of walking right in for a cup of coffee. But they wouldn't dream of interrupting you at golf.   HARPER LEE

ACCENTS & NICKNAMES

You'll find a few nicknames here and there, but nowhere, I'll venture, are they as common and well considered as in the South. One episode, one physical or mental aberration, one mistake, one peculiarity, and you get a nickname hung on you that will last for years.   ROBERT CORAM

Of all the Southern stereotypes, the one that answers to "Bubba" is probably least flattering. It speaks volumes about the sweet, good-natured, peculiarly Southern penchant for family nicknames. What other region regularly takes a child's inability to pronounce the word "brother" and hangs it joyfully around a family member's neck for life?

THE EDITORS, *Southern* magazine

The educated Southerner has no use for an *r*, except at the beginning of a word. MARK TWAIN

Apparently some believe that slow speech indicates slow thought—or so we might conclude from laboratory studies showing that the average non-Southern college sophomore assumes a Southern speaker to be less bright than a non-Southerner, even when the two are saying exactly the same thing.

JOHN SHELTON REED

'Cause we know in our culture that "people who tawk lahk thyat"—they may be bright, articulate, wonderful people—but people who "tawk lahk thyat are shitkickuhs." As bright as any Southerner could be, if Albert Einstein "tawked lahk thyat, theah wouldn't be no bomb." LENNY BRUCE

Southerners can probably say "shit" better than anybody else. We give it the ol' two-syllable "shee-yet," which strings it out a bit and gives it more ambience, if words can have ambience.   LEWIS GRIZZARD

Young feller, you will never appreciate the potentialities of the English language until you have heard a Southern mule driver search the soul of a mule.
                    OLIVER WENDELL HOLMES, JR.

Our country, south and west of Hatteras
Abounds in charming feminine flatteras.
Sweet talk is scant by Lake Cayuga,
But in Tennessee, they chatta nougat.
                              OGDEN NASH

Memphians don't speak English, they speak Memphish. . . . Memphish has taken the verb "like to" (as in "Sometime I'd like to return to the Big Apple") and warped it, astonishingly enough, into an adverb. It now means "nearly," as in "I liked to have died of embarrassment," which invents a whole new verb tense in the bargain.   ED WEATHERS

In Southern English, "naked" means you ain't got no clothes on, while "nekkid" means you ain't got no clothes on and you're up to something.
                              LEWIS GRIZZARD

Southern white speech drawls with ennui, frustration, and repressed hostility. The tensions of life in the South make most Southern women nonstop chatterers.   ASHLEY MONTAGU

MANNERS

"You all" down South is, in truth, the essence of courtesy. We never use it to mean "you" unless we are kidding. We may use it to one person, but he understands that we mean it in the plural, that we are inviting or including him and all his kin and friends. This subtle heart-outreach eludes our critics.

OREN ARNOLD

When you rattle off a standard Southern thank you—"Oh, you're just so nice, I don't know what I'd do without you!" the Northern man believes you! He believes you so much he follows you home.   FLORENCE KING

A joke going around down here asks why Southern women don't like group sex. Give up? Too many thank-you notes.   JOHN SHELTON REED

The South, with all the monstrous mythologizing of its virtues, nevertheless has these virtues—a manner . . . and a grace and a gift for human intercourse.   WALKER PERCY

A Southern woman finds it almost impossible to accept a compliment without depreciating the thing praised. It's as though she considers it immodest to admit that she possesses something really nice.

MILDRED JORDAN BROOKS

The South still has a better chance of working out its problems than the more urbanized rest of the country, simply because more of us still know one another's names.   WILL CAMPBELL

We say grace, and we say "ma'am."
If you ain't into that, we don't give a damn.

HANK WILLIAMS, JR.

People down South are incredibly polite. Even their war was civil.   DUDLEY MOORE

As somebody once observed, Southerners will be polite until they are angry enough to kill you.

JOHN SHELTON REED

Southerners are probably not more hospitable than New Englanders are; they are simply more willing to remind you of the fact that they are being hospitable.

RAY BIRDWHISTELL

They [the Japanese] are coming in droves, and *Tennessee Illustrated* has given a new dimension to Southern hospitality by publishing a list of handy phrases for its readers. *Haguki to hoppeta no aidani hitotsumami irenasai,* for example, means "Put a pinch between your cheek and gum." *Virusu wa sugoine* translates as "How 'bout them Vols?"

JOHN SHELTON REED

Virginia planters, each living on an estate without neighbors (though, it is true, with family, servants, and slaves for company) demanded nothing better than to receive strangers who could bring to them a breath of fresh life and news from the outside world.

The origin of Southern hospitality may well have been boredom.

WAVERLY ROOT and
RICHARD DE ROCHEMONT

There were some very conservative antibusing people, liberal whites, outspoken blacks, and so forth—mortal enemies, you might say—and getting them to associate with one another at all was a big problem. Our idea was to invite representatives of all the groups to a covered dish dinner, thinking that regardless of race or politics or whatever, Southerners have always been brought up to be nice at the table.

MAGGIE RAY

The South excelled in two things which the French deem essential to civilization: a code of manners and a native cuisine. JOHN PEALE BISHOP

YANKEES

The difference between a Yankee and a Damnyankee is that the Yankee had the sense enough to stay where he belongs.   BOYCE HOUSE

To the inhabitants of the Southern states, not only the New Englander, but everyone who dwelt north of the Potomac was a Yankee—a name which was with him a synonym of meanness, avarice, and low cunning— while the native of the Northern states regarded his Southern fellow citizens as an indolent and prodigal race, the comparison with himself but half civilized, and far better acquainted with the sword and the pistol than with any more useful instrument.

MARIA MCINTOSH, 1852

No lie, the average Yankee knows about as much about the South as a hog knows about the Lord's plan for salvation.   WILLIAM PRICE FOX

Some native Southerners still operate on the theory that a Yankee is worth more than a bale of cotton and twice as easy to pick.   JONATHAN DANIELS

THE CHANGING SOUTH

The required transformation will not make the Southerner into a warmed-over Yankee, nor deprive him
of those special, concrete ways of life that mark
Southern society. Instead it will let the Southerner use
his style of life to be with other men instead of apart
from them.   JAMES SELLERS

Hell, you talk about the *Gone with the Wind,* Sherman,
and the Civil War were only an illusion for all the
smoke and roar. This time, without anybody even
noticing it, it's really happening. The South is vanishing quietly as a passing of summer light—and this
time, for good.

    AN ATLANTAN, remark made to Marshall Frady

The South, which has gained so much in justice, has
lost a great deal of grace.   CHARLES KURALT

The South as a state of mind is expiring, and everybody is too busy building skyscrapers and making
money to notice.   DALE BUMPERS

All talk is dying. No more porch talk because no more porches. Air conditioning and television have taken us inside to be passive voyeurs of a fake world made in Hollywood and New York.   JOHN EGERTON

The South is becoming etherized in all those ways a people are subtly rendered pastless, memoryless, blank of identity, by assimilation into chrome and asphalt and plastic.   MARSHALL FRADY

The Southern past, the Southern present, the Southern future . . . became one of red clay pine barrens, of chain-gang camps, of housewives dressed in flour sacks who stare all day dully down into dirty sinks.

RANDALL JARRELL

Like the children of Israel, the people of the South have undertaken a Journey. The South is on the way to a Promised Land. . . . The pillar we follow is a vision of economic parity with the nation.

RUPERT VANCE

In our efforts to improve the South, we have often seemed to discard that distinctiveness and make the

South a carbon copy of the North. It is not too late to correct these mistakes and it is not too early to predict what will happen if we do not.

REUBEN ASKEW

When you travel through the South, you soon realize that despite the plastic and the interstates, the region is not in any immediate danger of being swallowed up by mainstream America. FRED POWLEDGE

The Vanishing South . . . has staged one of the most prolonged disappearing acts since the decline and fall of the Roman Empire. GEORGE TINDALL

The South is the future. It's the future right now. People say it's just a fad, but it isn't a fad. It's going to have a marvelous influence on this country because it will teach people to be much kinder to each other and more forgiving and more easygoing and more neighborly and simply more forbearing and genuinely more concerned about other people.

JAMES DICKEY

The thing about the South is that it's finally multiple rather than singular in almost every respect. You've

got to say about eight different things about each subject to say what it is, whereas before you could always
say just a couple. HODDING CARTER

A century is a long time. The Confederate flag is often
just confetti in careless hands now.

JONATHAN DANIELS

It's different now. The people down here in the South
now is got their shit together. Everybody's fine; everybody gets along beautiful, and I'm so happy that
that's what happened. But you can always find a
fool—you can find a fool in church, you understand?
BO DIDDLEY

I'll tell you something else and you can mark this
down as a prediction. You give this country twenty
or thirty more years, everybody's got any sense is
going down South. LEROY "SATCHEL" PAIGE

Many Southerners of a certain age . . . have moved
beyond the old defensiveness on the one hand, the old
guilt on the other. They don't object to portraying
the South warts and all—as long as it's made clear

that Southern warts are more interesting than anyone
else's.   JOHN SHELTON REED

Lots of folks in my generation who grew up in the
South have a kind of inferiority complex that we're
just gettin' out of.   CHARLIE RICH

The best thing that's happened, and in the past 10
years I think—and I believe people don't really realize
this—is for the first time in Southern history, for the
first time in 150 years, the South is no longer defensive. I mean for the first time since the revolutionary
days, around 1820 or '30, the South is not trying to
defend this peculiar institution or what followed it. I
don't think we realize how much Southern talent and
Southern brains went to defending this.

                                           WALKER PERCY

No more must the slogan of states' rights sound a
recalcitrant and defensive note for the people of the
South. For the era of defiance is behind us.

                 VIRGINIA GOVERNOR LINWOOD HOLTON,
                                   inaugural speech, 1970

I don't know too many people in the south who want to see a return to separate anything.

DOUG WILDER

[I see] a maturing South . . . a humanistic South, which has always been there, just below the surface of racism and despair, struggling for a chance to emerge.

REUBEN ASKEW

THE NEW SOUTH

There's Southern new and Northern new,
And one is warmer and funkier too,
And one has no fried okra at all.
And I know which, and so do y'all.

ROY BLOUNT, JR.

The New South will be an urban South.

THOMAS H. NAYLOR

Before and since Henry Grady used the term in 1886, every generation of Americans has been told that the South of its day was a New South.

EDGAR T. THOMPSON

For a generation now, the South has talked and written of a "New South." The birth pains are at last beginning. RALPH MCGILL, 1950

One of the first things I can remember in my life was hearing about the New South. I was three years old, in Alabama. Not a year has passed since that I haven't heard about a New South. I would dearly love never to hear the New South mentioned again. In fact, my definition of a New South would be a South in which it never occurred to anybody to mention the New South. WALKER PERCY

There is, in fact, no Old South and no New. There is only the South. Fundamentally as it was in the beginning it is now, and if God please, it shall be evermore. ROBERT COTTERILL

THE SOUTHERN IMAGE

Time and television, the two great cultural Cuisinarts, have done little to erode the myth of Southern differences, which for Northerners and Southerners alike has always exceeded even the facts of difference.

SHARON McKERN

A Southern is a movie in which the South, or at least the idea of the South, is integral to its personality, one in which the setting is more than mere background but, in fact, helps define your ideas about the story and the characters. As a rule of thumb, if you have to think twice to remember that a movie took place in the South, it's probably not a Southern.

CATHERINE CLINTON

Hollywood has always had a patronizing attitude toward the South. I couldn't sit through *Gone With the Wind,* it was so bad. There should be a line of guys with shotguns at the Mason-Dixon Line to tell actors, 'You can't come here unless you know what you're doing.'

ROBERT DUVALL

The tremendous impression which Miss Mitchell's Scarlett O'Hara made upon the Northern audience is owing to the fact that Scarlett is a type of ruthless entrepreneur which Northerners have met in their own life and can therefore understand and credit.

RICHARD WEAVER

The name Scarlett O'Hara may conjure up images of connivance and a tendency to live in the past but, hell, we've elected presidents who exhibit those qualities.   THE EDITORS, *Southern* magazine

When they [Southern writers] point to the fact that only a very small percentage of Southerners had plantations and owned slaves, they miss the point. The moonlight, the magnolias, and the dueling pistol did not have to be universal to possess validity, because it was all a state of mind anyway, and this often prevails against armies as well as statistics.

HARRY GOLDEN

There have always been two versions of the South, both wrong. On the one hand there is the *Gone With the Wind* South: bronze men in white linen suits, demure ladies with lace parasols, white-columned mansions framed by magnolias, courtly black butlers named Melvin, and gentlemen who make their own whiskey. On the other hand, there is the *Tobacco Road* South: sawmill towns, potbellied sheriffs, hillbilly singers, Jackleg radio preachers, tin-roofed chicken houses, and gentlemen who make their own whiskey. So you can see that Margaret Mitchell and Erskine Caldwell didn't totally disagree.   PAUL HEMPHILL

Dave Gardner never got around to organizing his National Association for the Advancement of White Trash, so it's still okay to portray Southern whites as amusing nincompoops.   JOHN SHELTON REED

I think it demarcates something new, but if we think it's the end of the *Deliverance, Gone With the Wind,* "Dukes of Hazzard" image of the South, I think we're being very optimistic.

EDWARD L. AYERS, Clinton election

Music

It is difficult to put over a joke about any of the Southern states. They go best in sentimental songs.

W. C. FIELDS

The "love" in country music is written in lower case; there is little refined about it. It wells up within us unbidden, and it is thick as tar and just as unwieldy.

CAROL F. WALL

Country music is a grassroots, foot-stompin', shit-kickin' music that deals in unvarnished reality rather than dewy-eyed romance. It's for grown-ups who've racked up some mileage.   SHARON MCKERN

With country music, if you can't understand the words, there's no point to it.   JOHN SHELTON REED

Country music makes America a better country.

RICHARD NIXON

Country music didn't begin in Nashville. It started up above Knoxville. Knoxville should have been Music City. Acuff, Scruggs, Flatt, Atkins. They knew what it was. Insurance money took it to Nashville, but the memory just isn't there. The memory is in those hills and eddies above Knoxville.   H. J. KUNTRY

Country music was always the folk music of the white Southern working class.   PAUL HEMPHILL

On Beale Street, where urban met rural, folk met jazz, and white met black, blues poured out.
          DENISE SCOTT BROWN

Some time ago, a geographer at Oklahoma State mapped the birthplaces of country-music notables . . . it shows that country music is Southern music. But they're not from just anywhere in the South. . . .

Country music is a product of the fringe, of Appalachia, the Ozarks, the Southwest. The Deep South appears as a near-vacuum. . . . But when one of my students did a similiar map of the origins of blues singers and we overlaid it on the country music map, it filled in the Deep South nicely. The two maps together clearly showed the South—black and white, separate but equal—to be the great seedbed of American music. JOHN SHELTON REED

I still like black music best of all. That's the root of all American music—Southern black music.

PHIL WALDEN

To me the South is unexplainable. All I can say is that there's a sweetness here, a Southern sweetness, that makes sweet music. . . . If I had to tell somebody who had never been to the South, who had never heard of soul music, what it was, I'd just have to tell him that it's music from the heart, from the pulse, from the innermost feeling. That's my soul, that's how I sing. And that's the South. AL GREEN

The Southerner talks music. MARK TWAIN

The South is the only place we play where everybody can clap on the off-beat.   ROBBIE ROBERTSON

Elvis

It was like he came along and whispered some dream in everybody's ear, and somehow we all dreamed it.
                                        BRUCE SPRINGSTEEN

When I first knew Elvis, he had a million dollars' worth of talent. Now he has a million dollars.
                                        COLONEL TOM PARKER

One small-town boy, born at the right time, in the right place, in the right environment, and under the right circumstances [represented the convergence] of all the musical currents of America's subculture: black and white gospel, country and western, and rhythm and blues.   HENRY PLEASANTS

This kind of thing can frighten a person: During Elvis International Tribute Week, I noticed three Filipino

Elvis impersonators mugging for photographs in front
of the duck-filled fountain in the lobby of Memphis's
Peabody Hotel. All three had on the requisite cos-
tumes—white bell bottoms and jackets, fringe all
around, armored sunglasses, shiny DA haircuts—and
as they posed, each of them tried on Elvis's familiar
sneer, curling their lips and glaring their hound dog
best into the lens of the Instamatic camera they were
sharing. And I didn't even give them a second glance.
You live in Memphis long enough, you get used to
the Elvis cult.   DAVID DAWSON

The Trophy Building is filled with gold and platinum
records, a gun collection, keys to cities and towns all
over the world, and a startling fashion statement: the
evolution of the jumpsuit according to Elvis.

                    JINX AND JEFFERSON MORGAN

The most striking item was a poster that showed a
tight-trousered, full-bottomed Presley playing a guitar
in the lower left-hand corner, with a staircase leading
up to his mother and Graceland—the Presley house
in Memphis—in the sky. Redneck fulfillment—socially pathetic at one level; at another, religious kind
of art, with Christian borrowings: the beatification of
the central figure, with all his sexuality, Graceland like

a vision of the New Jerusalem in a medieval Dooms-
day painting.   V. S. NAIPAUL

There's something significant in the fact that Elvis not
only began his career in Memphis, but that he lived and
died there. It's not just that his music pulled together the
various strands of the Southern sound and gave it a single, connected, powerful surge, but that he did it from
his hometown—and that it's hard to imagine him doing
it from anywhere else.   MITCHELL J. SHIELDS

NORTH & SOUTH

When the employer up North notified this fellow that
he was being transferred South, he went out and
bought a book *How To Make Mint Juleps,* and then his
wife briefed him on the South of *Gone With the Wind.*
The second day down here he wrote a "letter to the
editor" about the Supreme Court decision against racial segregation.   HARRY GOLDEN

An Easterner solicits the name of your school. A
Northerner wants to know what business you're in.

The first question most of us Southerners ask you, however, is, "Who was your grandmother, dear?"
                                    MARILYN MICHAELSON

A New York friend said that visiting the South reminded her of nothing more than being in high school again.   ROSEMARY DANIEL

What the North generally has done is to accept the social conventions of the South, while condemning the reasons for those conventions.
                                    BISHOP HUGH McCANDLESS

Northern blacks are Southern blacks. They just moved North.   ANDREW YOUNG

Northerners who are anxious to look elsewhere for explanations of increasing economic impotence at home too often seek refuge in simplistic reliance on regional prejudice. In short, they blame the South for the bleakness of the North.   E. BLAINE LINER

The fact is simply that for the North the South is too theatrical to be wholly real; therefore it is "history" and not "real life."   RICHARD WEAVER

Here's another rule for getting along in the South. If you must give unsolicited advice, pretend it's something that just occurred to you. Never, under any circumstances, tell us how it's done up North.

JOHN SHELTON REED

Can there ever be any thorough national fusion of the Northern and Southern states? I think not. In fact, the Union will be shaken almost to dislocation whenever a very serious question between the states arises.

SAMUEL TAYLOR COLERIDGE

The only reason people live up there, dear hearts, is because they have jobs there. Did you ever hear of anybody retiring to the North?

BROTHER DAVE GARDNER

The North excels in business, but the South leads in romance.   IRVIN S. COBB, 1917

The vogue of romanticism was not particular to the Southern states, but it attained a more luxuriant growth below the Potomac than anywhere else in America.

Clement Eaton

But let's think about that accusation: still fighting the Civil War. Non-Southerners are never accused of that, no matter what they say about the South. Neither are Southerners who make it clear that they prefer the Northern way. You get charged with that offense if and only if you are a Southerner who would like to see the South stay Southern.

John Shelton Reed

Well, I think the point is that the North is so preoccupied with its own difficulties that the Northern moralists are no longer concerned with the south.

Walker Percy

The North isn't a place. It's just a direction out of the South.

Roy Blount, Jr.

SOUTHERN EXPATRIATES

It dawned on me, after too many boring cocktail parties with too many terribly proper New Englanders, that what I was really missing at Harvard was the sweaty passion for life I had always taken for granted while growing up in the South.   PAUL HEMPHILL

The change from Alabama to New York had somehow disturbed her; accustomed to the idle warmth of a small Southern town, the matrix of the family and cousinship and childhood friends, she had failed to accommodate herself to the stricter, lonelier mores of New York.   CARSON McCULLERS

I am myself a writer from the South who has wound up in New England, an area that I find—generally speaking—more tasteful than Georgia, but less tasty.   ROY BLOUNT, JR.

And finally, one learned something about the nature of New York friendships. They were unlike any other friendships I had ever known. In Mississippi, or in

Texas, "friends" had been people whom one saw frequently and informally. . . . [In New York] one could call a person a "friend" if you saw him once every four or five months, talked for a while, and got along.
                                                    WILLIE MORRIS

In New York you may have the greatest and most congenial friends, but it's extraordinary if you ever know anything about them except that little wedge of their life that you meet with the little wedge of your life.   EUDORA WELTY

I was sort of disgusted with the South at the end of my stay at Vanderbilt. I was extremely provincial when I went to New York. I began to think that we had something here, after all, that I shouldn't let go of. I felt more and more strongly when I went to Europe. I think if I'd stayed in the South, I might have been anti-Southern, but I became a Southerner again by going East.   ALLEN TATE

Don't we all feel more Southern, and more affection for the South, when we're away from home?
                                                    LINTON WEEKS

As long as Southern expatriates criticize Northern society well, they can be surprisingly successful. Right many talented Southerners have been moved by living in the North to do exactly that, and the literature of American social criticism is richer for it.

JOHN SHELTON REED

Even today [the Southerner] seldom really abandons the South, no matter how wide his travels or how exotic his climate of sojourn. The very act of departure is too invested with a taint of betrayal, and already too weighted with the dream of return. Let a Mississippian reside forty years within mugging distance of Washington Square; still he will be no authentic New Yorker.

JAMES HARKNESS

True Southerners hold historical bonds and cultural bonds to the heart, above geography: They remain Southern wherever they are.

BILL NEAL

I came into this world in North Carolina, and I will depart this world in North Carolina.

CHARLIE ROSE

All Southerners go home sooner or later, even if in a box.

TRUMAN CAPOTE

Take me home. I was born in the South; I have lived and labored in the South; and I wish to die and be buried in the South.

BOOKER T. WASHINGTON, his last words

Index

About the Editors

JIM CHARLTON has written a number of books and edited several volumes of quotations including *The Writer's Quotation Book, Fighting Words*, and *A Little Learning*. He has collaborated with Ms. Binswanger on a number of projects including *Good Deeds, The Perfect Wedding Planner*, and their daughter Meg. Mr. Charlton, a native New Yorker, considers Memphis his adopted home.

BARBARA BINSWANGER is a book producer and literary agent, and, in addition to the collaborations with Mr. Charlton, is the author or co-author of four books on parenting. Ms. Binswanger has lived in New York City for fifteen years, but she will always call Memphis home.